Get ST

Get STAR
www.they ...g.publishing

Published by Get STARTED don't quit Publishing
Monty K Reed PO Box 65230 Seattle WA 98155 USA
www.theyshallwalk.org/publishing
copyright © 2012, 2019

$15.99US $20.99CAN €14.27EURO ¥1776JPY $22.50AUD £12.25GBP

ISBN 978-0-578-22041-3 $15.99

First Edition copyright © 2012
Second Edition copyright © 2019
ISBN 978-0-578-22041-3 (paperback)

Other books to watch for coming soon:

"Get STARTED don't quit STUDY GUIDE" $6.99US

"I Saw Angels" $15.99US about encounters with angels
www.ISawAngels.com copyright © 2019

"Have A Pity Party" $15.99US how to schedule anger, frustration, grieving, and pain for your success.
www.HaveAPityParty.com copyright © 2019

2

Get STARTED-don't quit!

Acknowledgments

Thank you to Stacy, for being my best friend, my wife, my love, my life. Thank you to Tony, Ciara and Isaac, for being my amazing children.

Thank you to all my friends and family for supporting my vision to give the gift of walking to the world. Because of you, there are over 300 paralyzed people who use powered exoskeletons today instead of wheelchairs. As well hundreds of clinics have exoskeletons to share with paralyzed people who want to learn to walk again. My dream is to make those exoskeletons available for over a million people who want and need them. Thank you to all the volunteers who have come and gone over the years, with a special thanks to the ones who have stuck around through thick and thin.

Thank you, David Moody, Doug Bell, Michael Shemet, James Mock, Les Neu, Chance Burris, Pam Miller, Randy Kaiser, Ted Walker, Dr. Steve Steins, Ron Warkentin, Cecelia Lehmann, Francis Nguyen and Charlie, Mark, Alice, Todd, Ben, Bill, Steve, Leo, Wade, Jeff, Don, Debbie, Bernie etc….

There have been so many volunteers over the years I cannot list them all here. There are so many sponsors and donors that I cannot list them all here either.

A special "thank you" to some of our biggest supporters:
NASA   Underwater Sports
University of Washington   University of Michigan
University of Saint Louis   Event Logistics of Washington
The Rotary Club of Vellore India & Rotary International
Boeing   City of Shoreline   Microsoft
www.Snackies.org   www.ditchyourphonebill.com

Names have been changed to protect the guilty
and the innocent.

3

Introduction

Monty is definitely God's Can-Do-Man. Many people, including instructors, and experts in their fields told Monty emphatically he will never be able to do many things. They painted for him a very sad, mere existence, picture of the things he possibly could do with his life. Monty has truly blown them away. He has not only accomplished more than the expert's expectations but exceeded their wildest imaginations. Monty is the perfect person to write a book about how you should Get STARTED-don't quit! Monty is the real deal and the good news is he's not done yet. You are able to glean from his personal testimony and journey in this book, the many miracles that happened to him and through him along the way by his not quitting. If you have ever had one of those days, or weeks, or seasons like the rest of us living on this planet; where obstacles rise up, difficulties are beyond your control and even sometimes people closest to us trying to convince you to stop, this book is for you. Sometimes people try to get you to quit because it looks hopeless and they tell you "no one in the history of ever has done it, so obviously you can't do it, so why try?" The answer is in this book. It's not hopeless and nothing is impossible. Monty has discovered the answer to success and a fruit-filled life with God's help. The answer is in your hands right now to give you encouragement and the inspiration to Get STARTED and don't quit. God has told us in His Word "I can do all things through Christ which strengthens me." Phil 4:13. "let the weak say I am strong." Joel 3:10. "and we will have a great harvest if we do not give up." Gal 6:9. You will be greatly encouraged by the true testimonies in this book. Watch your own life begin to completely turn around for the better. Begin to write down and keep track of your own stories as God helps you personally through this book
Get STARTED - don't quit!

Enjoy the Journey

Bernie Ferrell
Pastor for 43 years in the State of Washington

4

Preface

Why I wrote this book

While I was in high school the experts told me, my mind was not good enough for college. Today I have a college degree and I graduated with honors. A few years later while I was in a hospital with a broken back the experts told me my body was no good. Today on bad days I have trouble walking or getting out of bed. On good days I can ride my bicycle a hundred miles. Over the last three decades while sharing my story at events around globe, many of you had asked for my book.

I had written over 1000 pages in my journals detailing my travels over the years. There was so much material it was holding me back from actually writing a book. Then in 2012 I met with Ray Wilson (Black Buffalo, a native American) who was a speaker and prolific author. He was one of my favorite speakers to listen to. I had read a few of his books, they are short and easy to read. After one of his speaking engagements at Philadelphia Church in Seattle, I spoke with him about wanting to write my book. He encouraged me to write my book and just Get STARTED. He prayed with me and told me that I should write my first book NOW. In 2012 the first edition was published and sold out. You hold in your hand the second edition of my first book "Get STARTED-don't quit!" Thank you for reading this book.

A few years ago, just 17 weeks from when I had that meeting with Ray Wilson, the first edition of that book came out and was very well received. Many of the chapters from this book will become individual books over the next few years, so let me know what you want to read about next.

In April of 2019 I was blessed to go to Israel with my wife and while basking in the blessing of the Holy Land and

5

my father in heaven on my life, I wrote an additional 100 pages for this book. The cover is a photo I took on April 14, 2019, at the top of Masada the famous mountaintop fortress in Israel that is a symbol to the Jewish people to never quit.

April 15, 2019 in my hotel room in Jerusalem I finished the book and sent it to the printer. It is my hope that these stories will motivate you as it has the thousands of people who have heard the stories told by me in person. Now… Get STARTED-don't quit!

Warm regards, Monty K Reed

Second Edition copyright © 2019
Published by
Get STARTED don't quit Publishing
Monty K Reed
PO Box 65230
Seattle WA 98155 USA
http://www.theyshallwalk.org/publishing

Please feel free to let me know if you have any feedback
monty@theyshallwalk.org
(206) 250-5639 text, call and Whats App
This is actually my cellphone number and yes you can call me. Send a text to let me know what times work best for you or just pick up the phone and call.

www.MontyKReed.com
www.facebook.com/Monty-Reed-231805516856166
https://www.linkedin.com/in/monty-k-reed-b125489
http://www.twitter.com/MontyKReed
www.youtube.com/MontyKReed

Contents

Page

Contents

Chapter 1

Humble Beginnings: Cabin on the River Bend

My father told me stories about our first home, and he took me to visit when I was ten years old, during a summer camping trip. We rode in the car and after driving down an old dirt road, past a field of hay that had just been mowed (makes me think of Craig Morgan's song "Almost Home"). We parked the car and loaded up day packs with lunches. We walked down the railroad tracks about five miles and passed through a tunnel. As the light at the end of the tunnel got brighter, I could see the shack to the left in the center of a big green patch of grass, surrounded by a couple of fruit trees. It was on the bend of a river and looked like one of those antique paintings you find in old coffee shops or the walls of grandparents' homes.

As we got closer dad told us about the days we lived there. He was a new husband with two children and his job locations changed weekly because of the life of a railroad man. He was always a hard worker and that got him favor with his supervisor. Because of that favor and his hard work, he was given permission to occupy the unused conductors' shack on the river bend just outside of Great Falls, Montana.

In the morning we would have breakfast cooked on the wood stove that was fired by kindling dad chopped. The train would slow down in the morning and dad would jump on to catch a ride to work. At the end of the day he would jump off the train the same way he got on.

"today it would be called a tiny home and get on the cover of a magazine"

Many times, he would shoot grouse on the way home or he would simply toss a line in the river and pull out enough fish for dinner. Dad was always in the wilderness as a youth. Hunting, fishing, hiking and camping. I loved his endless stories of his

9

adventures in the Glacier National park and the Bob Marshall Wilderness area.

The shack had a tin roof, wood walls and dirt floors. There was a main room, a kitchen area and a bedroom. The kitchen was the wood stove, a wood pile, a counter with a water basin and pitcher. It was probably less than 500 square feet.

My father was always ahead of his time, today it would be called a tiny home and get on the cover of a magazine or a blog page.

After just two years on the river bend dad got an offer to work in the big city of Seattle. You can take the old boy out of the country, but you can never take the country out of the old boy. Dad listened to and sang country songs. He wore cowboy boots, bolo ties and jeans. Turquoise was for dressing up. In fact, the 'country' is so deep in our blood my daughter inherited it naturally.

The rest of my childhood was spent in Seattle. We did get to go to grandma's and grandpa's in the summers. Grandma and Grandpa Reed's house was the country living, cooking, hiking, hunting, fishing and outdoors grandparent's retreat. The Shannon's home was the culture, theater, arts, etiquette and breeding summer grandparent's home.

Chapter 2

My First Job and My First Business at Age Seven

Watching my father wake up early in the morning and sing while he got ready for work taught me that a job or career did not have to be toiling work. Work could be fun. I learned about a job by watching my dad go to work every day. He got up around four am every morning and began his routine. He always left early to beat traffic and if he got there early enough, he could get started on the job without delay. He would very often wake me and talk to me about things we were going to do that day and that week and encourage me to have a great day.

Reeds work hard and play hard. Many people have commented over the years that I "just don't quit" when it comes to work. Sometimes they have complained that my work ethic makes everyone else look bad. I was just trained that way by my father. I remember helping with the firewood and complaining a little. My complaining stopped shortly after it started because the complaints seemed to fall on deaf ears. My father explained that "You take a rest from chopping wood by carrying the firewood. When you get tired of hauling wood you can rest by chopping wood."

"When you get tired of hauling wood you can rest by chopping wood." Larry Reed aka Big Daddy.

My brother got a paper route and he let me work for him. He taught me about employee motivation by paying me at the end of the route right outside of the candy store.

Now I say "candy store" but it was really a "ma and pa" grocery store, however when you are seven, they are all candy stores. Safeway candy store, Fred Meyer candy store, QFC candy store etc... After doing the job for a few

11

weeks and trying out different candies with my hard-earned dime, I made an observation.

In this candy store, I discovered that there was a generic candy that just happened to fit in the Pez$_{tm}$ dispensers, and it was only two cents. At the time, a Pez$_{tm}$ refill was a dime. So, I invested my dime and bought five of those candies. It was hard not to eat the candy on the way home. When I got home, I went to the craft area and got out some paper, pencils and crayons to create a work of art and put private labels on the candy with tape and resold them for a nickel.

All the other kids were overjoyed at the idea of getting these Pez$_{tm}$ refills for half price. The first week I only made fifteen cents, and I re-invested it into my business to buy inventory. Soon I was selling a hundred candies a month. I had my own business at age seven. With that business I discovered the effects of envy and even experienced the rumor mill where other kids started to say I was stealing the candy and that is the only reason I could sell it for half price.

I had money I made from my job, and money from my own business.

I had to shut down my candy operation when we had expanded into gum and a couple of my sales reps had been caught at school. They turned state's evidence against me and blamed me for bringing the gum to school. When they gave me up, I found myself in the principal's office facing the paddle, facing away from the paddle, actually. I took my "lickin and kept on ticking. However, I am no fool, so I quickly removed gum from the inventory.

Gary Vaynerchuk was in Seattle on a book tour and I heard him say "If you never had a paper route or never had a lemonade stand and you own your own business, you'd better get a partner who did." I agree. Gary Vaynerchuk is one of my favorite authors and speaking personalities. When he was in grade school, he had basically franchised the lemonade stand idea and was riding around on his big wheel to collect the money from his multiple refreshment stands around New York.

When he was a little older, he sold baseball cards and was able to earn over $1000 a weekend. This kind of money made it hard for him to focus on school. Gary realized he made more money per hour than his teachers did so "Why would I listen to them?" I did not have that epiphany until much later in life. I continued to earn the business owner and employee types of income.

My friend Joe's dad's name was Ron, we were neighbors. Ron had a job delivering beverages for Coca-Cola bottling company during the day and at night and weekends he managed properties in our neighborhood and the nearby ones that he owned. As far as I could tell we knew he owned five houses that people I knew lived in. I learned about rental property from watching him. I saw how to take a three-bedroom 1920 style house and split the rooms with extra closets and turn that house into a rental with six bedrooms. I even helped a little with some of the work on turning a basement of a house into a mother in law apartment. Ron taught us how to turn a big old house into a duplex and triplex too by adding kitchens and baths to each floor and adding separate entrances.

I imagined I would own properties just like he did, and I would store my wealth in real estate when I was older. Turns out I was able to do a little of this with a big 1907 house in Ballard in 1990.

Chapter 3

No One Hits My Brother

I must have been eight or nine years old when I was playing across the street from my house. I used to climb buildings a lot to retrieve balls for my friends and had accumulated a very large unclaimed tennis ball collection. We did not have any tennis rackets so we would hit the ball against the wall with our hands, a sort of "street hand ball". I was playing alone and a couple of older boys in their teens came up from the rail road tracks. "Nice tennis ball, let me see it" one of them said. I handed it over. I didn't much care if they gave it back since I had a large collection. It was clear they were not really interested in the ball; they just wanted to fight.

Pretty soon they were on top of me, one holding me while the other kicked me and punched me. They hit me in the face, legs, arms, and stomach. It was hard to breathe, and my blood was getting into my eyes. Blinded by the sting of the saltiness of the plasma, all I could do was try to call out for help.

I took in the deepest breath I could between their blows and let out a call "Maaaaaaaaaaaaaarrrrk!" and again "Maaaaaaaaaaaaaaarrrrk!" a third time I cried out and then one of them put his forearm over my mouth to shut me up. I bit down as hard as I could and that only brought me more pounding from the both of them.

Off in the distance I heard footsteps running towards me; they sounded more like a bounding stride. Then closer, rapid steps as he came to a halt, one guy flew off me, then the other. I wiped the blood from my eyes and turned to see a sight of wonder.

My brother had the two on the ground next to each other. One of his knees was in each of their chests. He hit the one on the left with his left hand and the one on his right with his right hand as he yelled one word with each punch:

"No…One…Hits…My…Brother…But…Me!" again "No… One…Hits… My…Brother…But…Me!" and again "No…One… Hits…My… Brother…But…Me!" Faster and faster, more pounding, more yelling, until they were both bloody and still. Mark was gasping for air and let out a frustrated growl sigh sort of sound. The look on his face and his body language was like he was saying to the two silent assailants "Why did you go and have to make me do that?"

"Why did you go and have to make me do that?"

My hero helped me up and walked me back to the house. Halfway there I stopped and looked back at the two boys still laying on the ground, and then I smiled at my brother. I felt bad for those boys, but they may have killed me if my hero had not come to rescue me. Mark got me into the house and in the bathroom where most of our family first aid supplies were administered. He cleaned me up, got me some ice, put me to bed and brought me tomato soup and a grilled cheese sandwich.

We never spoke of it again until recently. I think at the time he did not want anyone to know how much of a hero he really was. He really is a great guy and all-American hero. Later he joined the United States Marine Corps and went for it.

Chapter 4

My Best Friend

An amazing thing happened that changed my life during the first grade. I met my best friend, one who would never leave me nor forsake me. I attended Catholic school formally for twelve years, unofficially for fourteen if you count CCD (Confraternity of Christian Doctrine) classes that I attended for two years before first grade. For those of you not familiar with the Catholic church think of it like Sunday School on a Wednesday night.

"I will never leave you nor forsake you"
Heb 13:5 KJV

One of the things I liked best about Catholic school was the bible reading time. Especially in first through fourth grade it was like story hour. On this special day, my first-grade teacher, Sister Pauline Carol, read from the Bible as she always did every day. She read to us:

"When thou prayest, enter into thy closet, and when thou hast shut thy door, pray to thy Father which is in secret; and thy Father which seeth in secret shall reward thee openly."
Mathew 6:6 KJV

I remember thinking to myself, "Dad never said anything about a prayer closet" and the wheels started to turn. I figured he never said anything about it because it was supposed to be "in secret." As only a first grader could, I began to imagine there must be a secret room somewhere in the house that was the prayer closet. I could not wait to get home and find it.

16

It seemed like I spent hours upon hours searching, yet it was probably, really, only about ten or fifteen minutes.

I looked in the back of the cabinets for false backs and bottoms hoping to find the secret panel that would lead to the secret prayer closet. At the time my brother and I watched a lot of Batman and Robin and the idea of a secret bookcase that slid open was alive and well in my imagination. In the TV show I remember there was a statue on the bookshelf that needed to be moved in just the right way and the door that was a bookshelf would open up and reveal the secret entrance to the Batcave, so I was looking for the same kind of controller for the sanctuary or prayer closet.

I was very disappointed when I did not find the prayer closet. I made up my mind that the linen closet in the upstairs hallway must be the prayer closet, after all it was the only closet, we had. Climbing to the top shelf, I pushed the towels aside, closed the door and began to pray.

"Within a few days I met the Holy Spirit."

Gifts of the Holy Spirit started to manifest as my relationship with him grew.

At that time in the Catholic Church these things, "the gifts of the Holy Spirit" were frowned upon when they manifested in the modern age. I was fortunate to have had a counselor, a priest named Father Conrad. When I asked him about the gifts of the Holy Spirit manifesting, he advised me to

"keep it just between you and God"

"keep it just between you and God, don't tell anyone around hear about it because a lot of them believe that all of the gifts of the Holy Spirit stopped when the original Apostles died." So, I did not tell anyone.

17

It was not until many years later when I met my wife that I found out there were Christians who spoke in tongues, interpreted the tongues, prophesied, praised God openly, and expressed other gifts of the Holy Spirit in public and at church on Sunday.

Today I am a non-denominational Pentecostal Christian who embraces the King James Version of the Bible as the true word of God. I also believe I have a relationship with the same God who was worshipped by Abraham, Isaac and Jacob; the same God worshipped by the Jewish people, I met in Israel. I worship the same God worshipped by the people I met in Kenya, Oman, Somalia and India. I believe that God the father sent his son, Jesus Christ of Nazareth, to live on earth as a human being. He did this so he could experience what it was to be human. I believe that Jesus had to rely on God the father for his miracle power as a lesson to all of us. Jesus died on the cross as the ultimate sacrifice to end much of the Old Testament law and begin a new covenant with all people who choose him.

You can do that too, if you do not know Jesus you can ask him now, right now, if he is real. Ask him to show himself to you. Ask for the Holy Spirit to speak to you and reveal himself to you.

I believe in Jesus as my Lord and Savior and for that belief God has granted me the gift of going to heaven when I die. I believe that Jesus left us a comforter that he called the Holy Spirit. The Holy Spirit is the presence of God that dwells on this earth and in me. Anyone who will accept Jesus and call on the Holy Spirit can have him dwell with them and in them.

This is the truth that I learned from the Catholic Church in first grade where I met my best friend, the Holy Spirit. The Holy Trinity is my Heavenly Father, Beloved Savior, and Holy Spirit. I have carried this truth, this friendship throughout the trials of my life. It has been this best friend that has helped me to face the tests in my life. I have witnessed people die and come near to death myself many times. I have seen the worst in people and with God's help I have made it through it all.

Many people I meet share with me how much they think I am strong to have made it through so many trials. I tell you it is not my personal strength, but my weakness and reliance on God that has made my journey look so easy.

When I knew that I was going to heaven, the worst thing I could imagine that would happen to me in my life is that I would die and go to heaven. With that pending fate it is easy to be positive about my future. I have seen God directly intervene in my life so many times there is evidence of God's presence and of the covenant I have with him.

When I pray, first of all, I thank God for all the blessings he has given me. I try to reflect on those blessings and what they really mean to me and my life. When I pray for a miracle or healing, I call on the Holy Spirit in the name of Jesus Christ of Nazareth. I ask God the Father in heaven for the miracle in the name of Jesus Christ and I ask the Holy Spirit to manifest the miracle or the answer to prayer.

"God always answers prayer."

God always answers prayer. Sometimes we do not like the answer, but he always answers. Sometimes he says "No," sometimes he says "Yes," and sometimes the answer is "Not now."

"Sometimes God says No"

19

Pastor Derek Forseth says it best and when I asked him, he told me he got the idea from someone else, so he does not take credit for this, I give him credit for it because it is the way he has always shared this.

"God always answers our prayers... Sometimes he says NO it's not my will, sometimes he says SLOW the timing isn't right, sometimes he says GROW because he wants us to mature while we wait, and sometimes he says GO because our asking is in his will." Pastor Derek Forseth

God's timing is not our timing. I thank God for my free will, and I ask him to accept it (my free will) as an offering or gift back to him. I ask God for his will in my life, what he would have me do to glorify him.

"Trust in the Lord with all of your heart." Proverbs 3:5 KJV

The hardest part is waiting on the Lord to answer my prayers. Sometimes he answers with a sign, sometimes he will use a man or woman of God who will speak to you confirming something God has already shown you or told you, sometimes a strong feeling and sometimes he answers with a vision or a dream.

I always tell people that being positive for me is not a choice, I have to be positive...it is in my blood. You see, it was on my dog tags too, I am blood type "B positive." Then I laugh. The reality is I have the joy of the Lord in me. As a small child, when I realized the worst thing that will happen to me is that I will die and go to heaven, well there really is nothing that can give me a bad day.

"Seek ye first the Kingdom of God and all your stuff will be okay."
Mathew 6:33 JKV...
Pastor Joe Knight version

Chapter 5

Free Will, Visions and a Coke Bottle

While still in the sixth grade, I had a dream that I died and went to heaven. You see I had spent most of my elementary school years trying to be a pacifist because that is one of the ways Jesus was described to me at the Catholic school and church. He turned the other cheek. I did not pay attention to the part where he got passionately angry at the money changers and flipped the tables over. Later, my advice to my children was to not take it to the extreme I did and look for a balance. Even Jesus only had one other cheek to turn, so consider that.

"Even Jesus only had one other cheek to turn"

I was young and blissfully unaware of the reality of the capacity for evil my fellow man has. If you ever want to find out, just ask the teachers and playground monitors from the local elementary school about the evils of the troublemakers. Ask your local law enforcement officer or read some international news about developing nations and the imbalance of power around the world. I'm just saying they are out there.

Since I was the local pacifist the local bully would beat me up after school. I was so extreme I would let them beat me up and then apologize for getting my blood on their clothes. The rule was that you could not fight on the school grounds. That meant on that city block the school was located on. If you crossed the street, everyone was free game as far as fighting went, so that is usually where scores were settled. My only score was zero for zero since I would not fight back. Some days the other bullies from the other schools would be waiting for me too.

22

In this vision I had, the bully met me after school across the street, on the corner by this big rock. In the dream he kept hitting me harder and harder and just went too far. I hit my head on the rock, died and went to heaven. When I woke up, I thought I was going to heaven after school so I was a little clingy with dad in the morning and a little bit on the "I love you" too much with my brother and sister that morning as we walked to school. I did not know you could change your future by implementing your free will. I thought if you had a vision, that is the way it is going to be.

While walking to school, I glanced over and saw an old Coke bottle partially covered in dried mud. Have you ever heard that still small voice, speak to you or urge you to do something? I felt like the Holy Spirit was urging me to pick up the Coke bottle. I did not want to. I remember thinking to myself as I felt God was urging me to pick up this dirty bottle: "Well at least you are not asking me to build an ark" and I picked it up. A few blocks later, across the street from the school, I felt God inspiring me to put the bottle down. Not just anywhere, but specifically behind the big rock where all the fights happen. I thought "That is a strange as asking me to pick it up in the first place, but you are God so, okay." And I put the bottle down behind the big rock.

Then after school the crowd was already gathering for my regular beating. The bully started up his warm up routine and I took the blows to my stomach, legs and face. I could see the bully from Hamilton middle school (the next closest public school) in the back of the crowd warming up for his turn. After only a few minutes the bully from our school hit me a few times just like in the vision. The same exact punch, and kick as in the vision. I was reliving the dream and I thought "Here we go, I'm coming home to Jesus" and then just as quickly things changed. He hit me in the face, and I started to fall toward the rock, and I twisted a little as I went down. My head did not hit the rock, as in the vision but

23

instead I landed across the rock and there I was looking at the Coke bottle I had placed there a few hours before.

I was never going to hurt anyone, I was mad, and my body ached. I grabbed the bottle and smashed it on that rock and started screaming using a prayer language that sounded unintelligible. I pointed the jagged sharp edges of the broken bottle at the bully that had just knocked me down. He looked at me like he had never looked at me before. The way no one had ever looked at me. His eyes were big, he was scared. I imagined that was the way I usually looked when they were beating on me.

I jumped towards him and waved the jagged glass bladed bottle at him. He jumped back. It felt good; I felt a surge of power. I did it again and he lurched back, almost tripping as he got out of my way. Then I lunged at the bully from Hamilton and yelled out more and waved the broken glass. The whole crowed cleared out and I headed home.

I realized the concept of predestination no longer worked for me. I had used my free will to change the outcome of what I had seen in a vision. The vision was there to warn me, so I did not die. I was forever changed.

Going forward I forever realized that visions are there sometimes to help us to avoid a potential future. God may show us a vision of things that may be to come. Free will is so powerful and it is a gift we all have. You can use your free will to change your future. Decide what it is you want out of life and decide to ask God to help you get it.

24

Chapter 6

A Dearning Lisability Known as Lessdyxia

A Dearning Lisability Known as Lessdyxia. This is a term I have coined and used many times. In case you don't get it, it is a play on words using poetic license and it is designed to make you see what people with learning disabilities see with many words. This is the disabled version of Learning Disability Known as Dyslexia. (copyright 2019 all rights reserved by Monty K Reed)

"You are not going to college." she said to me. I was devastated. I had always wanted to work in a lab. I wanted it so bad since I was a child that my father took one of his old white dress shirts and sowed it into a lab coat for me. I had envisioned working in the lab and inventing things. Always, I was drawing pictures of inventions and imagining building things. I imagined working for Jacque Cousteau in a marine biology lab on a ship.

I had a 1.86 GPA and needed to do extra credit just to graduate from high school. Some classes I had earned 4.0 and others failed miserably. Zoology, Botany and Architectural drafting were 4.0 classes (A+). My history and English teachers were frustrated because the rubrics (scoring system) they had to grade me, required they mark me down for punctuation and spelling. This was before word processors or the internet. I had a couple of them tell me if it were not for the errors the paper would have gotten a B+ or an A. The spelling and punctuation were so bad that I got D and F grades on most of my papers. My participation in class made it obvious that I was listening during lecture and that I at least looked at the books. My reading level was about a fifth grade during high school and it was painfully slow. The pictures, captions, figures and charts helped me a lot.

25

Three teachers really believed in me and encouraged me more than others. My English teacher went so far as to allow a little artistic license with some assignments. After failing an exam, she decided to offer me a chance to retake the test orally. I got an "A." Then she allowed me to do a book report on George Orwell's "1984" by drawing a series of pictures as a book report and I got another "A." The next book report she let me do an oral presentation to the class instead of written work.

Back then, when you wanted to look things up, there was no internet. In order to apply to colleges, you did not go to the website, they had no websites. I had to go to the library to get addresses and write letters to colleges requesting admission forms and course catalogs. After six to eight weeks I received piles of literature from many colleges. Narrowing it down to three took a little work but, I did it. I found three that had great marine biology programs.

"you're not going to college"

When I met with the high school counselor, I thought she was going to help me apply to these colleges. You know, fill out the paperwork and maybe even apply for scholarships. I did not know she was going to tell me what she said. She said, "You don't understand… you're not going to college." She continued "have you seen your scores or your grades? You have to look at other options for your life. You could be a fisherman in Alaska or consider being a janitor at Boeing." Now I will say this… there is Nothing wrong with being a janitor or a fisherman, if that is what you are called to. I was not. I was called to wear a lab coat.

I stood up and walked out of her office. She had some brochures in her hands, I think they were Boeing and Fishing boat brochures, I don't know for sure. I left that big stack of

26

material I had brought in from the colleges and walked out. My dream of wearing the lab coat were crushed. She was the expert, I did not know then what I know now, that I did not have to listen to her. I could have chosen to ignore her and go for it.

Many years later at the University of Washington I had asked to get into the engineering program so I could study robotics and I wanted to do it without doing any college math. That went over like a lead brick.

"Yet because this widow troubleth me, I will avenge her, lest by her continual coming she weary me." Luke 18:1-8 (Read the whole thing its better)

Thirteen people told me "NO!" I kept asking like the widow who went before the judge. What do you know? The fourteenth person I asked said "Oh yes we have a program that is actually designed for people just like you, under self-directed degrees." I attended with honors. I became a NASA Space Grant Scholar and a Mary Gates Scholar.

Bill Gates mother was a regent at the University of Washington and to honor her, he set up the Mary Gates endowment with a forty million-dollar ($40,000,000) donation. The money is invested and any money above the original endowment is given away every year in the form of scholarships. Today there are just around four thousand Mary Gates Scholars in the history of ever. I point this out, not to say I am amazing, I point this out to encourage you. Think about it, I was told "you're not going to college" and I became an honor student on full ride scholarships. You can too.

After getting the bad news, I still really wanted to do something more with my life. I investigated a lot of jobs. My senior year I investigated being a police officer, firefighter,

27

ship engineer, and becoming a travel agent and that looked good. I could not find any starting positions with a travel agency.

The other option was to take a job with the airlines. After writing letters and a phone call, an interview was scheduled. The representative from the airlines came to my home to interview and even met with my father. The pay was great for the time. One of the benefits that I was going to take advantage of was being able to travel for free to wherever the airlines traveled on my days off.

"A news story changed everything."

I imagined I could do research and write articles and books about my travels around the world. They had a retirement plan that my dad said was very good. The major retirement benefit that I was interested in the most was a credit card with the airlines name on it that would allow me to travel where ever they flew at no charge.

After the interview I got the job offer. I was seriously considering the job; I was planning on a career in the airlines.

A news story changed everything.

Chapter 7

Ranger Reed Get STARTED

In my senior year of high school, I had been practicing being a better passivist because I was trying to be more Christlike. A car bomb went off in Europe and twelve women and children were murdered. The story wrenched my heart. The rest of the news report was about the five or more groups that were trying to take the credit for the murders. This was my introduction to terrorists. Their mode of battle was so contrary to the knights of old England that I had studied while learning about armor, courting and chivalry a few months before. The mindset was so "anti-gentlemen" so inhumane I snapped.

The standard operating procedure for terrorists was to kill ten to scare ten thousand. Horror was the tool they used, and they always would prefer to attack civilian targets. Preferably unarmed and defenseless women and children. Almost always, healthy young male terrorists murdering women and children. What kind of creature would be so spineless and so evil?

I had postulated the word "devil" was a combination of "de" and "evil" ~ "the evil" or "the evil one." Could I have discovered "the evil ones?" I realized the terrorists are not the devil himself, but it was obvious they were not worshipping the same God I was. They claimed to be doing God's work. It is clear and obvious to anyone who knows the God I serve that they were not doing his business because he is a God of love. Terrorists were doing the work of an earthly god, a fallen angel, or the god of this earth.

"the god of this age."
2 Corinthians 4:4 KJV

29

Demons influence them and trick them into believing they will be rewarded in heaven for murder. They will be rewarded by the god they serve in his kingdom with the fires down below. I imagine the terrorists who blow themselves up spend eternity experiencing the pain of that explosion over and over and over.

At seventeen years old, I wanted justice for those people who were murdered and for their families. Marching downtown Seattle to second avenue where all the military recruiters' offices were; I started at the south end and walked into the Marine corps office.

"I want to fight terrorists"

"I want to fight terrorists" I exclaimed after introductions were out of the way. The soldiers in the office smiled at each other then back at me and explained that I had to join up, do the best I could, work hard for years and if I were lucky, I would be selected. I was told I could not sign up to fight terrorists directly. I had to volunteer and hope I would get picked.

Inquiring "Are you sure?" I was looking for a different answer and they did not have it, so I went one door North to the Coast guard office. There they offered me a chance to hunt for drugs and contraband on ships. The Navy recruiters told me the same thing about being selected as the Marines had. The Navy Seals had to select me; I could not select them. I thanked them and continued on my quest. Next was the Air Force recruiting office. There I learned about the Pararescuemen soldiers, and that sounded like a pretty good job, yet, it was not the mission I was looking for.

When I walked into the Army office the man behind the desk was smiling. I suspect the Marine Corps guys had called to let him know I was coming. "I want to fight terrorists" I announced just as before. The difference was the recruiter's

30

reaction. With a smile he held out his hand to welcome me. After a few minutes he basically told me "You hold the pen, I'll move the paper, boy. We have just the place for you, Airborne Rangers at Fort Lewis Washington."

"You hold the pen; I'll move the paper"

A few days later I was at Fort Lewis meeting some of these modern-day heroes. They were all kind gentlemen types with a strong conviction to protect America and every freedom and ideology it stands for. Sergeant Slater was one of the Rangers I met who was especially patriotic. He told me about the mission to train for war, being ready and praying for peace.

Since I had heard rumors that military recruiters don't always tell the whole truth as far as what your assignment will be and how long you will be doing it. I actually had the recruiter's office produce a contract that said if I would score one hundred percent on all my testing and qualifications, I would be assigned to the second Ranger Battalion at Fort Lewis (2_{nd} BAT Ranger $2/75_{th}$).

If you wonder what kind of a "Goody Two-Shoes" I was in high school, I must tell you that I was no saint. I tried the best I could to be Christ like, however, I am just too human to be all that. I realized, as a human being and a man, I had a capacity for evil because of my free will. I had to choose a life that could help guide me. What I was looking for was a way to be constrained into being a better person.

At a younger age it was signing up to be the crossing guard captain in seventh and eighth grade with Steven Brumble. As the crossing guard captain in training I had to live up to a greater standard. In order to be in charge of a bunch of goody two shoes, I had to be the ultimate goody two shoes.

31

Steve and I both had to be accountable to the higher standards, in the public eye at least.

Scouts was another way of being accountable to a group of people that would hold me at a higher standard so my free will would be kept in check. Becoming an altar boy was another fellowship and discipline that helped to guide my principals.

Law enforcement explorer scouts was one avenue I took to guide me. My senior year spring break, while my friends were at parties in Fort Lauderdale and in Mexico, I was at the US Army Base Fort Lewis, at a two-week mini Police academy. I learned basic law enforcement and how to shoot a pistol. I was honored to be elected the Vice President of the class.

I decided I would win the shooting competition. I had been practicing meditation and relaxation with a little breathing and focus exercises. It was like martial arts without the "woo woo." The scriptures say I am to "Meditate on it daily." When it was my turn to shoot, I took a deep breath, moved my arms inward towards my body with each breath in a sort of Tai Chi move and reviewed every second of the one-hour class we had on shooting. All of these words flashed through my head in a few seconds before I fired; "Breath in… V grip on the handle, sight picture, heartbeat, muscle tone, squeeze, confirm target, squeeze some more, don't fight the kick of the gun, relax, relax, relax,…" By the time is was over I had beaten everyone and won the top shooter award.

All things are possible through Christ Jesus who strengthens me, and you. Jesus said when you ask for anything on earth it will be done in heaven. It must be good; you can't just ask for a million dollars and he will give it to you. He is not a piggy bank or a genie. There is a lot more to it. You need relationship with him. With that relationship you have rights and responsibilities. Because of my covenant with him I had the right to ask that I win that competition. Because I was fulfilling my responsibility by TRYING THE BEST I COULD to obey the ten commandments and the beatitudes of Jesus.

I was in the military Delayed Entry Program (DEP), where I had signed all the papers while I was still in High School with a pending ship date of November 1, 1983. The week before I was scheduled to leave for basic training some American medical students were being held hostage in Grenada. Sergeant Slater was one of the Rangers who lost his life in that rescue. When I left for basic training everyone thought we were going off to war. It was a bit scary, but the benefit was that a lot more people quit than normal because the service was still an all-volunteer Army. The fact that we were in a conflict with soldiers on the ground ensured that soldiers who completed training were more likely to be committed to watching my back.

Some minor injuries during basic training and airborne school were easy to ignore because of my contract, I had to maintain a perfect score to be assured the Ranger assignment. I will share the details of those injuries in another book.

This contract required me to Get STARTED-don't quit.

Chapter 8

Ranger Reed Leader

The first day of basic training we pulled up to the barracks on these old charter busses. They reminded me of the Greyhound busses that I rode with my Grandmother when I was twelve. She had purchased a two week pass that allowed us both to ride anywhere Greyhound travelled. She and I visited all over the USA and Canada. It was a great time. I wish they would bring that bus pass back.

The drill Sargent walked onto the bus and introduced himself and told us it was his job to make sure we had a comfortable stay while we were there and that we had everything we needed. It reminded me of a tour guide on the first day of an adventure tour. The speech was surreal, something was just not right. He was being too nice. Then it happened…

His voice raised with every syllable and went from zero to sixty or a loud barking yell. "and you have thirty seconds to get off of my bus NOW!. One, Two, Three, Four." Everyone was in shock, I was in shock, what to do? I mean he was standing in the doorway. There really was no way to get off of the bus and yet he was getting closer to the thirty second mark. I had no idea what he was going to do when he got to thirty, but I did know I was not going to be on the bus.

I looked up and saw the red emergency exit handle on my window and pulled it in the direction indicated. "Fourteen! FIFTEEN!" He was getting even louder. There was a low pop and I heard the exact same sound all around the bus. The others were following my lead. There were a few guys pushing past the drill Sargent and he was yelling at them for touching him. "How dare you touch me you maggot, get down and do pushups!" Young recruits had their feet on the chair backs, and they were doing pushups on each other. The road block in

34

the front of the bus was impossible. "TWENTY-TWO, TWENTY-THREE!"

The back-emergency door was open now and guys were piling out as fast as they could. I dove out my window head first and rolled just like I learned from my friends, Mike Lazner and Don Gaffney when we were sparring in martial arts sessions.

I was running for the line that the drill sergeant had told us to line up on and there were drill sergeants everywhere stopping everyone who got close to the line. I was doing pushups and one of the drill sergeants kept yelling at me. I would do pushups, get up and start to run and they would find another excuse to get me doing pushups again. ..

After all of the recruits finally made it to the line the drill Sargent explained how we were to line up in formation. We got it wrong and we had to do pushups over and over and over again. Finally, we got it right.

"this would be the one second in my life that made the difference"

The next few minutes changed my military career. It really was less than a second that made the change, it was when I reacted to a question. The way I reacted and what I did that made all the difference in the world. In my world. If you have ever read one of those Sci-Fi books about parallel realities this would be the one second in my life that made the difference in how I turned out compared to other timelines or other parallel universes with unlimited possibilities and unlimited Monty's.

The drill Sargent said "Now that we got you in formation, which one of you is going to come up here and take charge of this sorry bunch of lost souls? I know I wouldn't want to." He said. "NOW, I need one of you to come up here and stand in this box" as he pointed to a blue, twelve-inch, square box that was painted on the cement.

I moved before I knew what I was doing, and I was standing in the blue box. I put my hand on my forehead in a sad attempt to salute the drill Sargent. "Private Reed reporting for duty sir" I yelled from the depth of my diaphragm as I had learned in drama at high school.

The Sergeants' eyes got big like the rabid dog I had faced down a few years before. He looked like he was going to kill me. "Don't call me sir, I work for a living, that is Sargent to you. My first name is Drill and my last name is Sargent. Got it? Good. Now get down and give me some pushups."

Sweat was forming on my brow from all the pushups. "You are the Platoon Guide; you will guide the platoon. I will tell you what to do and you will tell them what to do, and we will see how long you last." He went on to explain that the Platoon Guide is like a combination of the officer in charge of the platoon and the Platoon Sargent (the enlisted leader). In the army the officer provides the book knowledge for war and the enlisted Platoon Sargent provides the street smarts for battle.

Because we were all newbies in basic training, we got to be both for the training exercise. One of the things I noticed right away was that the drill sergeants were trying to use peer pressure to cause fighting amongst us. Part of the instructor's job is to get recruits to quit now during training so you will not have them quit on the battle field when lives will be lost over it.

As the leader I felt a responsibility for my men or "My People" my friend Yossi from Israel would say. The Drill Sergeants (DS's) would look for a soldier who would make a mistake and sometimes punish the whole platoon. Another tactic they used was to catch someone from a platoon, my platoon, who had a uniform failure at the formation before chow (going to eat food in the cafeteria). They would make us wait while the recruit was doing pushups. As soon as that guy was done, they would "Gig" another person from the same platoon. My platoon was gigged so many times in the first week, on one particular day when we finally got to go in for chow, we had only three minutes. As the Platoon Guide, I had to be the last one to eat too. On that day I did not eat. I yelled at my men to only look at their plate and only grab food they could swallow without chewing; mashed potatoes, meatballs, gravy, split pea soup, etc... "Grab two glasses of milk and wash it down and get out so the rest of us can get in there and eat"

I yelled at the guys and they did what I told them, it made sense. And because I did, and they did we all got to eat. Well I did not eat that day and it was okay. The value of me missing dinner so all of my people could eat got me respect from all of the the men in my platoon as well as the others. I had a knack for leading. I have a way of figuring things out, I can only explain it because I trust in the Lord and the Holy Spirit speaks to me with his still small voice.

It seemed like the DS's were always trying to break us. I realize now there were a lot of men on my team, in my platoon that I should have let quit. I just did not have enough experience to know who those guys were. The next day, after I had missed my dinner, I called a meeting before the meeting with the men and told them I had a plan to beat the DS's.

"United we stand, divided we fall"

"Who here is tired of the Drill Sergeants getting the best of us?" I yelled. The crowd cheered with agreement. "I have a plan to show them we are real soldiers, I call it United we stand, divided we fall." I went on to explain "It will be hard at first and it will seem like we are doing more pushups then ever at first. Trust me, we are all going to do a lot of pushups anyway. We are going to kill them with kindness. Here is how it works:

37

whenever anyone from our platoon is called out or gigged and has to do pushups, anyone in our platoon who sees any one of our men being punished with pushups you all will have permission to call out as loud as you can "United we stand, divided we fall" and at the moment we will all drop to the pushup position and do the required pushups with our platoon member. This will build our team spirit and the drill sergeants will no longer have power over us with the pushups. Now let's try saying it together. No pushups right now, let's just say it together.

"United we stand, divided we fall"

We practiced four times and then we did it with the pushups. It was beautiful. Later, I had a couple of guys form the Bronx and Michigan complain about the idea, but they came around when they saw how well it worked.

Later that day one of our guys was late getting to the formation and he got called out by one of the DS's. As he hit the floor to do pushups I yelled out "Platoon, att-eeeehn-tion, repeat after me: United we stand! divided we fall!" then I added quickly "drop and give me twenty."

Everyone in my platoon took a step away from the center of the formation and dropped like one of those blooming onions for the Australian steak house restaurant. We counted together as we did the pushups, just like in PT (Physical Training).

The way we counted twenty pushups it was really twenty of the "Two Count" pushups. You say "One" as you push up and you say "Two" as you come back down to the ground, then you say "Three" as you push up again and you yell out LOUD "ONE" as you come back down to the bottom of the push up. So, you just did two pushups but they count as one pushup. There was some regulation put in place because of some lawsuit by the

ACLU or UCLA (Lesdyxick joke here) that the DS's could only make you do twenty pushups at any one time. There was no rule saying they could not make you do multiple sets and they decided if we had to do two count pushups than they would have the power they needed to teach and discipline us. I am glad they had that power. I wanted to have people who could handle it watching my back when we were done with the training.

After the first week the drill sergeant made me do pushups and put someone else in charge of the platoon. He lasted for one day. We were at a camp site and the DS put me back in charge. Later that week he called me into his office and asked me what my plans were for the military and I told him I was going to get 100% on all of my testing and I was going to be assigned to the Ranger Battalion at Fort Lewis. Also, that I was planning on doing a full twenty years and moving up to Delta Force. He was very pleased and told me the Army needed good men like me and to keep up the good work. He confided in me that I was one of the best platoon guides he had ever seen and was surprised that I had not served in ROTC. He said I was a natural.

"I will need to give the others a chance to lead, and when they mess up, I will put you back in charge so be ready to be the ongoing platoon guide. You will go far in this man's Army."

I wanted to give him a hug and of course I could not and would not. That just would not be appropriate.

Chapter 9

Ranger Reed Instructor

MP5SD Explanation, Demonstration, and practical application.

Figure 1 Monty Reed Ranger in the Middle East

Basic training, Advanced Infantry Training, Airborne School, and Ranger Indoctrination Program (aka RIP) were next, one after another. I watched the instructors and learned from them as they taught and led us. My RIP class started with 83 people that had come all the way through all of those other courses with me. Except for two who were added from some other

40

active duty units. From the eighty-three who started only thirteen graduated. At that point we were issued the Ranger Black Beret. At the time only Rangers had Black Berets and they had to be earned by completing the RIP course. Today it is a different story, all army soldiers are allowed to wear the black beret.

On the first day of being assigned to the Ranger Battalion, I was assigned to Sergeant Ide's squad with one other graduate from RIP.

Sergeant Ide growled "You two take a look at each other and just make up your minds now who will be here in a few months because one of you is going to quit." I could not stop myself and I just said to the other guy "You are the one who will be quitting, not me." He and I had just gone through a lot of the same "flaming hoops" to get to the Ranger Battalion and to be standing in that room. We were only together during the previous four weeks and prior to that he and I had been earning our invite to stay at different locations.

We had gone through basic training, AIT (advanced infantry training) airborne school all before the invitation to the RIP (Ranger Indoctrination Program) at Fort Lewis. During basic training and AIT we had seen a few people quit and a few get injured. Airborne school was different in a huge way. Every class was three weeks long: Ground week, Tower week and Jump week. Over eight hundred people started in my class. I brought with me a dislocated shoulder from the pugil stick training. Typically, the eight hundred people would whittle down with injuries and people quitting every hour.

"If your parachute does not deploy you will reach a terminal velocity of one hundred and twenty miles per hour. Do you know what happens to the human body when it impacts with the ground at that speed?" The Black Hat instructor was yelling out within ten minutes of the of the first class of the

41

first day of Ground week. "Do you know?..... well let me tell ya, it is not pretty, in fact it is pretty gruesome what happens." He continued a little louder "If your parachute fails to deploy and your reserve fails you will make contact with the ground at such a speed that the bones in your feet, ankles and your legs will all shatter at the same time." Lowering his voice he went on "the bone fragments will pierce your muscles and cut through your skin and clothing causing such internal bleeding and external hemorrhaging that you will die a slow agonizing death,..." Louder now "If YOU'RE LUCKY you will die quickly; if you do manage to survive it is very unlikely you will every walk again."

Figure 2 Runway at JBLM formerly Fort Lewis where I kissed the runway after parachuting in from Honduras with my fellow Rangers

He was leaning forward at this point. He stood up straight and with a gentle smile he quietly asked, "Does anyone want to quit right now, so you don't have to risk shattering your

42

bones and bleeding to death?" He continued "Just step over here and we will get you a hot cup of coffee and some jelly donuts for anyone who wants to quit." People moved in droves to the coffee and jelly donuts table where they got the delicious treats and were whisked out of the room. That was not the last time I heard that little speech.

To myself I thought "Get STARTED-don't quit!"

Figure 3 picture of a fellow Ranger I took just after landing in the jungle of Panama. Look below him you will see his rucksack on a strap

"Anyone want to quit?" was what I heard in my mind; "One of you is going to quit" is what I heard Sergeant Ide repeat and that brought me back to the here and now. I decided it was going to be Decker and I told him so.

43

I fondly remember Private Decker, he was a friendly guy the couple of months I knew him, even after he was declassified and had to turn in his Ranger uniform in exchange for the standard Army BDU (Battle Dress Uniform). It was considered shameful to be leaving the Ranger Battalion and anyone who was wearing the BDU while living in our barracks usually could not wait to get shipped out. Private Decker was a different breed. He enjoyed the fact that he no longer had to suffer under the leadership and "tyranny" of Sergeant Ide. He even told me he felt sorry for me. This next part of the story is for Decker.

In the afternoon we had our briefing and Sargent Ide tossed the manual for the sub machine gun at me. "Reed you are teaching the class tomorrow." That night I devoured the book and made my note cards. I also reviewed a couple of other weapons manuals to be ready for questions. I was going to be teaching all day and each class would have 30-100 people in them. I had to become the expert on this weapon so I could be trusted as the instructor.

The armorer, Landes, was a friend of mine and I checked out a couple of the MP5SD submachine guns and the armorer's manual. No one is supposed to even touch the book unless they are a certified armorer and I was not. I assured Landes I would not disassemble beyond field stripping. He did show me everything he know about the MP5 and it helped.

The next day, I yelled out to the class "This is the MP5SD sub machine gun; it is manufactured by Heckler and Koch of Germany. Today you will receive an explanation, demonstration and practical application of the MP5SD Sub-machine gun."

A couple of minutes into it a hand was raised. I had not even really started the class. It was Sergeant Ide. "Reed, can you tell me the contents of the silencer."

44

It was hard to hold back the laughter as I took in a deep breath to answer the question. You see, in addition to the manual on this weapon, I had become quite fascinated with the device in question and had just read a book about the history of the firearms suppressor that I had purchased mail order a few months before and I reviewed that book in preparation for this class.

"Thank you for asking that question, Sergeant Ide. First of all, I would like everyone to make a note that there is NO such thing as a SILENCER; that is a HOLLYWOOD term and only exists in the movies and in your DREAMS."

It was hard to keep a straight face as I continued "The MP5SD has attached to the barrel a Suppressive Device, hence the acronym SD." I looked directly at Sergeant Ide who was clearly upset and ready to speak out, so I talked faster. "The sound suppressor was invented by Hiram P. Maxim in 1908 when he was teaching his son to shoot on his family farm, and he was sensitive to his neighbors' peace and quiet. Mr. Maxim was familiar with the way automobile mufflers worked so he went to his workshop and the sound suppressor was born. It was patented in 1909 and sold in hardware stores." I barley took a breath and continued a little louder now.

"Back to your question, Sergeant Ide, about the contents of the silencer. As you now know there is no such thing as a silencer. The suppressors over the years have been built in several different ways and the dampening material contained between the baffles has been composed of several different things. Heckler and Koch has the SD listed as a non-serviceable expendable device and so I have not been authorized to disassemble the suppressor and therefore do not know what the exact contents of the SD are. However...."

Another quick breath and I continued "Most nine-millimeter firearms sound suppressors are manufactured with baffles and dampening materiel between the baffles and an opening down the middle so the bullet will pass unobstructed.... The most common dampening material to be loaded in the baffles is either steel wool, asbestos or fiber glass." I continued with a little about improvised suppressors and then looked at the Sergeant.

"Now, does that thoroughly answer your question Sergeant Ide? Do you have any other questions?"

"No Private Reed, that will be all."

If there was any doubt of the existence of God and the power of the Holy Spirit to arrange things to make me look good, this was one of those times. I could have never planned on reading the book about the history of the sound suppressor for firearms that would have prepared me to stave off questions from someone who was trying to make me look bad.

Instead, I got the upper hand and was able to thoroughly answer the question.

Figure 4 My Squad of Rangers in the Middle East

Figure 5 My Squad of Rangers in Central America

www.GetSTARTED-dontquit.com

Chapter 10

Friendly Fire and Fallen Heroes
WARNING: this chapter has graphic details of bodily harm.

I carried a pager back then, aka beeper. For the millennials and younger readers, this was a device that had one function and that was to deliver text messages. It was the size of your grandmothers flip phone and you could not return the text. You would pick up a land line telephone or use a payphone and call the number on the pager. When the pager went off, I had to drop everything and go back to work. It only happened a few times. Once in a busy theater in Tacoma my pager went off and over thirty other pagers were going off at the same time. A platoon size group of Rangers were watching the movie Ghost Busters and we all had to walk out of the movie.

"See the world" was a slogan that matched military service. Rangers traveled all the time. We had to be ready to be deployed to any environment in any part of the world at any time. We had to always stay within 24 hours of Fort Lewis when we traveled. We would spend a week at Fort Lewis doing laundry, repairing and replacing equipment, training and packing. Usually three weeks a month we were deployed somewhere.

We were immunized for every disease on the planet because we may have to go at any moment. We trained for all environments: desert, arctic, mountain, jungle, beach, foothills, rainforest and on and on.

When I first walked into the rec room at the Second Bat (Second Ranger Battalion) I remember seeing a wall map of the world, it had to be over twenty feet wide. "What are the red flags?" I asked. The red flags were hot spots where conflict was taking place at this moment. Bullets were flying

48

in over a hundred places on the globe. Places I never heard of and some places where I thought the fighting was over. Over the next couple of years, I visited over half a dozen of those spots.

Some of the most memorable were; Somalia, Panama, Honduras and Oman. You never really know what you are capable of until the rubber meets the road or the "fecal matter hits the oscillator."

While in Honduras on a routine training mission, we were approaching the target that was a few hundred yards away. We had been patrolling the wilderness of Central America for a few weeks, sometimes in the middle of the night and at times, like today in the middle of the day. Usually we would "prep the objective" (Prepare the objective to be assaulted) with artillery or mortar rounds before attacking. This was a training exercise so "what is there to worry about" I thought as we crept nearer to the target.

We had with us a new "butter bar" lieutenant (his rank insignia was golden, or butter colored). He was fresh out of OCS (Officers Candidate School) and he was excited to make a name for himself like most officers are. We had been on a couple of training exercises so far and this was his first time with us out of the USA.

"Fire for effect! fire for effect!"

The new Lieutenant called in the grid coordinates to my friends from the "weapons platoon" that handled the mortars. The familiar pop of the mortar tubes going off as they were supposed to was fine. The next sound was not good, not good at all.

"Fire for effect! fire for effect!" the Lieutenant repeated into the radio. Something was wrong. I was too new to

49

understand just how wrong it was, but I could feel it in the air.

My friends who worked with the mortars interpreted that call a little differently because this was a training mission. What they heard the Lieutenant say was… "Fire every mortar round you do not want to have to carry back with you." These men had to carry the mortar rounds on their backs to the firing position.

A dozen times before I had heard the mortar tubes in the distance and then the familiar sound of the live rounds passing over head toward the target. This time I heard a flickering, tumbling, twisting sound that was directly overhead.

You see the SOP (Standard Operating Procedure) for a simple mortar drop like this is to fire three rounds, see (with your eyes) where they land and if you miss you make adjustments to hit the target, then when you were close you could call "Fire for effect" or you could fire more test rounds. Never, I mean NEVER do you call "Fire for effect" before the test rounds hit unless you are being overrun.

I felt the hand of God in play. The closest person to me was over twenty-five to thirty feet away. I was wearing a t-shirt, a jungle fatigue shirt, a harness full of gear. There is no way any other human being could have touched me in that moment. As I was trying to decide which direction to run there was flesh on my flesh pushing me from behind. An angel in human form had pushed me, his bare hands on my bare back under my clothes and web gear. He pushed my face into the mud we were standing in. I know it was an angel because there was no man closer than ten meters (twenty-five to thirty feet) from me. Two bare hands contacted my shoulders from behind. The flesh was on my flesh under my web gear, my jungle fatigues and under my t-shirt. God intervened to protect me.

50

When mortar rounds hit the ground, they explode up and outward. The best place to be when they are hitting all around you is as close to the ground as you can be, and I was because of the angel's intervention.

"Wham-Kawoosh!" "Wham-Kawoosh!" "Wham-Kawoosh!" as one round after another hit and exploded. "Wham-Wham-Wham Kawoosh-Kawoosh-Kawoosh!!" as three in a row went off. Mud, rocks and grass landed on my back as I hugged the ground trying to sink into the mud. I took a breath as my mouth and nose went below the mud.

Fire for effect is an order telling the weapons platoon to fire all the rounds they had. Since this was a training mission and my friends did not want to have to carry any of the mortar rounds back to base, they were sure to fire every round they could.

Everything went silent after the first five or six explosions. I could still feel the concussion of the explosions. The first two were fast and then everything slowed down. I could hear and see things happening everywhere. I can almost remember hearing the mortar round hit, the fuse trigger, the primer fire, the and the explosion erupt. I may have imagined it, however. I only heard it on the first two rounds then those sounds were gone because of the deafness that had set in.

The whaming and kawooshing had stopped as I looked up. Smoke everywhere and a couple of small fires. I ran to the first body I found. There was only a boot and a piece of twisted metal where the soldier had been standing.

I was in shock since I had never seen a person turned into a puddle before. As one of the EMT's (Emergency Medical Technician's) I thought I was prepared. The ABC checklist was running in my head and none of it applied: "Airway,

51

Bleeding, Circulation… ah…hmm.. NOT here" my thoughts continued.

"Nothing I can do here." I thought matter a factly and with little emotion. In this type of situation everything slows down, and emotions are stuffed by the overwhelming rush of adrenaline. I ran from body to body to do what I could. Craig, Dunn, Bennet, and a few others were hit by shrapnel. Broken legs, sucking chest wounds blood and bandages everywhere. The smell of vaporized bone and burning flesh seared the air.

The nightmares started that night and three decades later they are a familiar friend, like a roommate you do not get along with that you cannot get rid of.

There are other stories of my brave band of brothers that others have told, and I do not have time to go into here. I will mention one man I will never forget having met.

"Dad do you know any heroes?" my son asked me a couple of years ago. "I did know some." As I started to answer his question my voice cracked. "in fact, I used to work with a lot of them." I cleared my throat and grabbed some water. While sitting my son down to tell him about the Rangers I knew. I had mentioned Slater earlier, the most impressive was Randall David Shughart who used to be my roommate.

Sergeant First Class Randall David Shughart was in Somalia in 1993 when a couple of Blackhawk Helicopters got shot down. Watch or read "Black Hawk Down" for more details. Shughart requested to be inserted with the crashed pilots to protect them while logistics was trying to medivac them. They were injured and could not get out on their own. Thousands of locals were descending on the crash site to tear the soldiers, limb from limb and burn them alive if they could.

Sergeant Shughart was denied his request several times while he was on a helicopter with a sniper rifle inbound to the crash site. I have been told the pilot saw hordes headed to the site. A third time he requested to be inserted. When he was asked if he knew the danger of this mission and that he knew he may not be getting extracted. He said he knew, and he was willing to fight to protect the downed pilots. He was inserted, fought his way to the pilots and then fired every round he had to defend them. He ultimately gave his life to protect those pilots.

"His actions saved the pilot's life. Sergeant First Class Shughart's extraordinary heroism and devotion to duty reflect great credit upon him, his unit and the United States Army."

http://www.history.army.mil/html/moh/somalia.html He

was awarded the Medal of Honor posthumously.

*"mission top secret destination unknown....
don't even know if we're ever coming home. "*

Army marching Cadence excerpt

*"misery, oh misery,
a Ranger life's a misery....
misery, oh misery,
a Ranger life's a misery....*

*Don't you cry me no tears,
I don't want your sympathy,
I'm an Airborne Ranger
and that's all I wanna be,
That's all I wanna beee,
that's all I wanna be,
I'm an Airborne Ranger, that's all I wanna be... "*

Ranger Marching Cadence song excerpts.

54

Chapter 11

The Accident

It was late at night and several hundred US Army Airborne Rangers were jumping (with parachutes) from the planes. It was a training mission over a field just outside of a place called "Schwäbisch Hall" in Germany. We were jumping from 800 feet to simulate conditions in which an anti-aircraft gun emplacement might shoot us down, just like the 1983 Grenada air field capture operation. We were jumping both doors of the aircraft which usually resulted in a variety of mid-air collisions leading to injuries. I avoided collision with other jumpers on all my previous thirty-eight jumps... However...

Figure 6 Rangers Parachuting

55

After my parachute opened, I noticed a lot of other paratroopers in the air that I needed to steer left and then right to avoid. Suddenly my canopy had closed. It was clear from the training I had, that some other Ranger had come under my parachute and stolen the air. At that point my canopy collapsed, and I began to free fall again.

The training taught me that I may be able to get the parachute to re-deploy if I shook the lines (risers) vigorously and I was over four hundred feet in the air still. I was only one hundred feet up so, I hit the ground before being able to reopen my parachute. My ankle broke, my low back and then the mid back broke in a couple of places. I blacked out. When I came too it hurt to breath. I thought I was bruised and did not know how badly I was broken. I figured "If I had broken my back I would be paralyzed or dead." I could walk a little. I figured it was not broken and I was wrong. The pain in my ankle was pretty intense so I found one of the medics. He taped my ankle and my torso. We both thought I was just bruised. The doc gave me some Ranger candy (combination of Ibuprofen and other medicine). He helped me tighten my gear around my waist and we marched through the woods eight miles to the helicopter extraction point.

The next day I could hardly move and reported to "sick call" where I was treated in Medical tent number two with heat packs, ice and more medication. We were in the field and still we all thought I was just badly bruised. The Ranger creed ends with.. "I will complete the mission though I be the lone survivor." That attitude was taught, embraced and even required for anyone who wanted to be and stay a Ranger. The doc kept giving me all the meds I could take but soon, I was an "unserviceable piece of equipment." I just could not hardly breath. Even with Percocet and Vicodin the pain was unbearable.

Figure 7 Ranger Monty K Reed taken in Central America

57

Chapter 12

The Hospital

Soon, I found myself shipped off to a hospital at Fort Ord, California just outside of Monterey. I was checked into the Silas B. Hays Army community hospital and moved to the fourth-floor West ward where I had a great sunset view of the ocean. My mattress had a wooden slat 'back board' that was covered in vinyl and had a single sheet over it. I was placed in traction and started on physical therapy twice a day.

I was in so much pain that I would usually stay up late-night watching television. The army hospital at the time had basic television, not cable, it was just a few stations: 3, 4, 5, 7, 9, 11, 13 and one UHF channel. When I had watched the original movie "The Planet of the Apes" twice in one week I realized I had been there too long and started to read books. My learning disability had not been diagnosed at that point, but I knew that I had always had problems with reading, spelling and math since the fifth grade.

That hospital had one 'candy striper' who worked for the American Red Cross. I cannot remember her name but today I can still see her face and her great smile. She would bring books, magazines and games around to all of the patients in the hospital. Soon I had read every book she had.

After a couple of weeks, I got transferred to the sixth-floor West ward (6W). The head nurse was really a 'dragon lady' she was mean and went overboard on the 'lights out' policy. Since I watched TV or read late every night I was affected

58

when she threw the breakers to turn off the lights and the TV at 9pm.

I could not sleep from the pain, my only peace came from prayer and trusting in the Lord. He did not heal me of the pain, he just comforted me in suffering through it. God has given me an endurance to push through the pain.

When the pain was so intense it was hard to breath, I would look up to the heavens and call out to God. "Please dear God, in the name of Jesus Christ of Nazareth, please heal me, take this pain from me, make me whole, healthy and well. I ask you Lord God almighty, please heal me." This has been one of the longest lessons in patience because God has chosen not to heal me of the pain. I do believe he has answered my prayer every time. I believe God has been telling me "Not now." He has given me the endurance to push through the pain. God has also given me a persistence that is beyond understanding

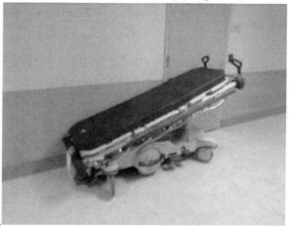

Figure 8 Hospital Gurney

59

Chapter 13

The Escape from the Dragon's Lair

"Yea, though I walk through the valley of the shadow of death, I will fear no evil: for thou art with me; thy rod and thy staff they comfort me." Psalm 23:4 KJV

One of my roommates, Blake, from the fourth floor had a surprise for me.

I was reading by flashlight in my room on six west when I heard a very faint squeak at the doorway to my room. I looked over and saw a wheelchair slowly rolling into my room with no-one in it.

Then another wheelchair appeared behind it. It seemed to be pushing the first one. On closer examination I could see my roommate from four west hunkered down low in the wheelchair so as not be be detected. He smiled and pushed the wheelchairs over to my bedside.

Together we got me into the empty chair, and he showed me just how to sit very low in the chair and not fall out. We started our escape adventure. Since the dragon lady had turned out all of the lights on the ward except the lights at the nurse's station, we were able to hug the walls and stay in the shadows for the most part. The biggest trick would be getting past the actual nurse's station.

Fortunately, the old nurse's station in that hospital was a bit taller than the traditional desk height so when we hunkered

60

down low in the wheelchairs, we were less likely to be seen. My chair did not squeak so bad with my body weight bearing down on the wheels but there was an occasional squeak and we would freeze and listen to see if the Dragon had stirred. We slowly snuck past the nurse's station and then the biggest hurdle... the elevator.

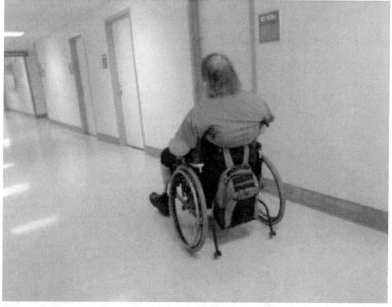

Figure 9 Escaping Down the Hallway of the Hospital

We pushed the button to go down, it lit and made no sound. We readied ourselves to race into the elevator and escape. The plan was for him to go first so he could hit the button as I was rolling onto the elevator car. We were going to the lobby.

"DING!" rang out as the red down arrow lit above the elevator door. A loud crunching roll opened the door and we raced into action. As planned, he hit the "L" button, I rolled in and we prayed. It seemed like forever as we waited for the elevator doors to close. A scraping sound tore at the silence as the Dragon stirred, sliding her chair back from nurse's station. Then footsteps. I made a mental note that she came down the south hallway towards the elevators. She was not running but she was walking quickly. We repositioned our wheelchairs as close to the walls of the elevator as possible, in case she rounded the corner before the doors closed.

It seemed like we were going to be caught… when the doors slid shut. My roommate had been pushing the "door close" button the whole time but it did not seem to matter. He kept his finger on it now to be sure the dragon could not tear open the doors. Alas, we were safe.

As the doors opened to the lobby I thought "what about the night guard?" Oh well, at least we had escaped the darkness of six west. We rolled out into the lobby and looked around. Fresh air was just minutes away if we could manage to escape the hospital. I motioned for my room-mate to be still and listen. We heard someone talking. As we rolled toward the door, we could see the night guard was talking to someone on the telephone. We slowly, quietly rolled out the main entrance as if we were supposed to. We hid in plain sight.

We made it; we were outside. It was a beautiful warm night and it was calm. The sky was clear, and we could see the stars. We raced around the near empty parking lot for what seemed like hours, though it had only been about forty-five minutes. It was about one fifteen in the morning.

As we finished yet another wheelchair race, we notice a car, a police car. The MP (Military Police) officers inside looked at us, looked at each other and got out of the patrol car. Walking up to us with flashlights drawn, one of them asked What we were doing in the parking lot in the middle of the night. I forgot to mention, we were wearing our hospital pajamas and gowns so answering their question had only a few creative answers as possibilities. My friend Blake, looked at me, I was thinking "he got me out of the hospital, so I need to get him out of this."

I coughed, then hacked, putting my hand, then both hands over my face as I coughed one more time looking deeply into my friends' eyes. He covered his mouth and hacked and coughed. I cleared my throat and said "Doctors orders, we were to get some fresh air, we picked up tuberculosis while on deployment" coughed, hacked and coughed again. My friend chimed in with more hacking and coughing, he even produced a bunch of phlegm to be more convincing "it is very contagious, don't get too close."

The MP's could not have been older than twenty, one looked like he was eighteen, he might have been. They both stopped and took two steps back. The one on the right put his hand up with his fingers spread out as if he was signaling "STOP" as I rolled my wheelchair a couple of inches towards them.

I continued "we are just supposed to be out here for another fifteen minutes and then we will be going back inside to quarantine." They got back in the car and drove off. We did not stick around, as soon as they drove off we headed back into the hospital.

We waited outside for the guard to move. When he got on the phone that was our signal, and as we had gone out we came back in like we owned the place.

The other surprise my roommate had for me was that the fifth-floor East wing was under construction. When he told me, I remember thinking "So?" as I looked at him with a puzzled look. He continued "The power is still on." Again, I looked at him with the "So?" stare. He finished with "The TV works, you can watch your shows." We raced to the 5E (fifth floor East Wing). The rooms had plastic up, painting, sheet rock, plumbing and wiring going on all over. On the North side of the building there were a few rooms with beds and TV's that were working. We watched twilight zone and a variety of other TV shows.

The remodel went on for over a month and during that time I was able to sneak out after lights out, every night to watch my shows and read my books. Returning to the dragons' lair on six west before sunrise.

Chapter 14

Matt Dillon of Dodge City

After being assessed for surgery with scans, x-rays, and other tests I was faced with a dilemma. As a US Army soldier in the hospital I did not have patient rights, legally I was a piece of equipment that was damaged and needed to be repaired. I wanted to be repaired but I was unsure about this medical system that did not even ask my opinion. After making several calls to attorneys in Seattle, San Francisco, Chicago and Washington DC I had to accept the fact that I really had no say in how I would be treated.

The ward had two attending physicians and they had the same rank. Normally this would have been no problem, but they both had different ideas of how I should be treated and what surgery I should have. It really was a power struggle on their part. I am sure they both believed they had the best track for my recovery. I just wanted them to fix my broken body so I could return to duty. I had committed to this path and was planning a lifelong career as an Army Ranger. I was going to at the very least put in my twenty years.

He said he had
"been doing surgery since Jesus was a baby"

Because they both could not agree on my treatment, I found myself in the office of the Chief of Orthopedics. He was old and he told me so. He said he had "been doing surgery since Jesus was a baby." I was a little offended at the way he threw around the name of my Lord and Savior, but he was just trying to make a point that he had had a lot of experience.

65

The humor was more important than my religious convictions, I needed some laughs. I got it. I asked him "which surgery I should have?"

"I've seen a lot of surgeons, got their scalpel in their holster like Matt Dillon of Dodge City..."

Something came over him, he got up from behind his desk and walked over to the open door of his office and closed the door. He slowly walked back to my side of his desk and sat down looking down at me. He raised his finger in front of his face. I felt like I was about to be scolded by my grandfather. He began to speak "son, I've seen a lot of surgeons, got their scalpel in their holster like Matt Dillon of Dodge City..." he paused.. "don't let them cut you with a knife." The look in his eyes was sad, tired and angry. Veins were popping out on his forehead and his neck. He was angry. Then he took a deep breath, dropped his hand to his side.

Then he continued "you are in the granola bowl of the world down here in California, it is full of fruits, nuts and flakes, you got Chiropractors, meditation, massage, acupuncture and all kinds of other stuff out there you can try. Try it all." He took a deep breath and continued "you are a patient, be patient, while they practice on someone else."

With that he got up and walked over to the door, opened it and came back to his side of the desk where he sat back down and looked at me. With his hands folded on top of his desk he said "son, what do you want to do?"

I chose not to go to Dodge City and get cut by Matt Dillon (Matt Dillon was the sheriff in a television show called "Gun

Smoke" where gun-slingers shot it out a lot. My new nickname for surgeons.)

Good thing too. Shortly after that I experienced a miracle healing and could walk without surgery. The chronic pain has never gone, and I still deal with that today. Some days all I can do is lay in bed and cry. Other days I ride my bike as far as 100 miles in one day.

*"you are a patient, be patient,
while they practice on someone else."*

Chapter 15

Visions of the LIFESUIT Robotic Exoskeleton

While I was still hospitalized, I read a book by Robert Heinlein "Starship Troopers" where the soldiers had powered armor that allowed them to carry over two thousand pounds of equipment. It was a lot like the Iron Man suit from the comic book. I had dreams about powered suits that allowed paralyzed people like me to walk. The dreams were really visions. The sights and sounds were extreme. I could hear sounds off in the distance, I could smell things and see things like they were real.

"your young men will see visions" Joel 2:28 KJV

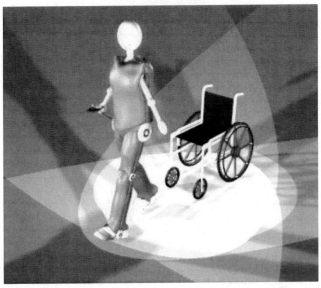

Figure 10 LIFESUIT Powered Exoskeltons Help Paralyzed People to Walk

68

In the first vision was of a man who was working as a framer on a house. He was up on the second story of the building swinging a hammer. He slipped and fell to the ground outside. Men rushed to his side to see if they could help. He was not bleeding but he could not move. The cell phones were a bit different that they were using to call for the ambulance. The cars and clothes were a bit different too, so I assumed this was taking place in the future.

The paramedics stabilized him by strapping him to a back board. Then they hauled him to the hospital where he had surgery. In the vision I saw him in surgery and followed him to his room. People came to visit, and he was stabilized within a few days. A man came into the room and measured him in the way a Taylor measures you for a suit.
Pretty soon he was being fitted with special bracing that had motors and a computer system. It was attached to his body with hinged door panels and inflatable padding.

It was a LIFESUIT robotic exoskeleton: robot suit.

Over his ear was clipped a device that looked like a single ear phone with a microphone on it. It looked very much like a standard blue tooth ear piece you would buy for your cell phone, however, in 1986 I had not seen anything like that. There was a piece that went forward but it was not a microphone. At the end of the rod was a sensor that pressed up against the temple and tapped into the motor function area of the brain by scanning for brain waves that would show up when a person was trying to walk. It was a device I call a Lobe Node.

I watched him go through physical therapy and occupational therapy where they taught him to use the LIFESUIT to walk, sit, stand and even dance. He learned to use it in a lot of work settings too. There was a mock up city inside the hospital where they had a simulated theater, post office, restaurant, house, retail cashier station, and a car. I watched him learn to get in and out of a car, go to the movies and use the LIFESUIT to work the cash register.

The paralyzed man simply thought about walking the the Lobe Node picked up the brain waves and the LIFESUIT walked, carrying the wearer with it.

In that first vision the house framer went home walking. He walked around the house and in a couple of days he was back at work, framing houses again. In the vision I could see inside of his muscles and nerves where his body was learning to function again. In that vision he needed the LIFESUIT for about two years and then he just learned to walk again. Living his life in the LIFESUIT gave him the gift of walking. He got STARTED and did not quit.

"In that vision he needed the LIFESUIT for about two years and then he just learned to walk again"

The second vision was a bit further into the future. In this vision some cars hovered, and some rolled. Building materials looked different, and the architecture was sleek and futuristic looking. A man was walking his dog as I looked on. He was hit by a hover car as they crossed the street. He too was rushed off to the hospital. The surgery went more quickly because machines, robots, assisted in the procedure. The LIFESUIT he was fitted with was a lot different. It looked

70

very much like a wetsuit a SCUBA diver from Underwater Sports would wear. The LIFESUIT was thin and was zipped onto the wearer. The technology was so affordable and so prevalent that his dog was outfitted with a zip on LIFESUIT as well.

He and the dog were walking again a couple of days after the surgery. By wearing the biosynthetic nanotech muscle fiber LIFESUIT for just two years the man and his dog were able to learn to walk again. They were completely healed.

As I looked into the fabric in my vision, I could see that the thread moved, it looked alive. The future version of the LIFESUIT was made from a new material that had not been invented yet. The fibers combined living muscle tissue with synthetics. I called them "biosynthetic muscle fibers." In the vision I could see super magnification of fibers so small the naked I could not even see them. I saw in a lab where thousands of valves, hoses, wires and electronics could fit on the head of a pin. Because of this tiny plumbing and control system it was possible to wire and plumb living muscle tissue to synthetic life support systems to create a symbiotic biosynthetic organism.

Later my technology would be featured in a textbook "Textile Futures" where they talked about my "Biosynthetic Muscle Fiber Clothing."

In that same lab I saw biosynthetic photosynthesis as well, where plant tissue and synthetic machines were connected. Animal waste was piped into the plant tissue, converted by the plants and animal food was piped out of the plant. The

71

application I saw in a later vision was in the mission field, deep sea excursions, NASA space missions.... These biosynthetic food pods were able to convert human waste into food because of the symbiotic relationship of the machines and the living plant tissue. See the section: Futurist Papers at the end of the book for more information about this.

After I awoke from each of the visions, I grabbed some paper and a pen and began to write as fast as I could. I drew sketches and recorded everything I could, especially the things that made no sense. I had visions every week for the time I was at Fort Ord (almost a year). I had forty-two visions of the future during that time.

My doctors had no hope for me. I was told my condition was permanent and it would get worse. I was told to accept my condition and my new life. I did not want to, and I did not. Instead I said to myself "Get STARTED-don't quit!." I prayed, prayed again and prayed some more. I called all of my friends that I know went to church and asked them to pray for me. I wrote letters requesting prayer.

As soon as I wrote down the basic vision and drew the simple sketches of what the LIFESUIT was and how it would work I was healed and able to walk. There was a purpose for my having the accident in the first place. I thank God that I can walk.

"Ask, and it shall be given you; seek, and ye shall find; knock, and the door shall be opened to you" Mathew 7:7 KJV

Chapter 16

You Got the Wrong Address Buddy

After the first two visions I had a pretty good idea of what I needed to do over the next forty years. In order to take the fiction out of the science fiction I needed to learn: Mechanical Engineering, Electrical Engineering, Computer Science Engineering, and Material Science Engineering. I also would need to learn about Robotics, biology and bioengineering. I felt like God wanted me to do this.

At first, I designed the robotic suit for myself. It was based on the Robert Heinlein book "Starship Troopers" where he described a powered armor that allowed soldiers to lift over two thousand pounds. In the book the powered armor had sensors inside that would detect the wearers movements. Heinlein described an array of micro switches all over the inside of the tank built for one. When the soldier moved his hand up it would hit switches inside the gauntlet of the armor. The switch would tell the computer to tell the motors to move the armor around the hand up. When it moved the pressure on the switch from the hand would be relieved and the released switch would tell the computer to stop moving the gauntlet up.

These micro switches all over the inside of the powered armor would simply notice when the body was moving and then move the armor out of the way.

In the same way the powered armor would walk, run and jump. Whenever the wearer would move the sensor switches would "feel" the pressure of the soldier and the armor would

74

move out of the way. Heinlein also described some special switches that were inside the soldiers' mouth and operable by the chin. All of these systems sounded like they would work on a robotic suit. I believed it and started to work on it as best I could.

I figured I would have the robotic suit working soon just like Heinlein's powered armor. I was going to build a Mimic and Playback system to go with it. The way I envisioned the system working was that I would put an able-bodied person in the powered suit and add a recording device that would feed information into a computer. I would get someone to wear the suit and do all of the things I wanted to do like walk, dance and exercise. After recording all of the movements I would create a library of the recorded movements and play them back to control the suit.

The robotic exoskeleton was going to give me my life back and so I called it the LIFESUIT.

I started to doubt that I was the guy to do this. When I started to look at my qualifications compared to what credentials I needed to have, I realized that there may not be enough time in my life to learn all of that stuff. Let alone building the thirty-six LIFESUIT prototypes, invent new materials, create the new science of biosynthetics, work with NASA, research at the University of Washington, train doctors and distribute the LIFESUIT robotic exoskeleton to all of the hospitals and physical therapy clinics in the world.

"And there came an angel of the LORD, and sat under an oak which was in Ophrah, that pertained unto Joash the Abiezrite: and his son Gideon

threshed wheat by the wine-press, to hide it from the Midianites." Judges 6:11 KJV

I felt like the angel of the LORD had come to my hospital and sat on the edge of my bed to give me an assignment of freeing people of paralysis. Some doubt crept in.

"You got the wrong address buddy." was my response to the angel of the LORD when he came to me with this assignment.

"You got the wrong address buddy."

I responded a lot like Gideon did. In his story the angel of the LORD had addressed him as a mighty man of valor and that he would save Israel from their enemy the Midianites. Gideon argued with the angel that his family was the poorest in their village and that he was the least of his family.

My argument was similar; my family was not affluent; my father was a single dad, and I was the least qualified in my family. My brother Mark learned electronics in the Marine Corps, my sister Alice was at college with honors pursuing a double major and I was a disAbled airborne Army Ranger who knew how to shoot and blow things up. Before joining the army, I had a fantasy about going to college. When I had picked out the three colleges I wanted to go-to because they had great marine biology programs, I was told by the high school counselor "You don't understand, you are not going to college. Your grades are not good enough to apply." She asked me, "Have you seen you SAT scores?" So, I am wondering how God is going to use me as an engineer to build a robotic suit

76

system that will allow paralyzed people to walk, when I cannot even apply to attend a college.

My extreme lack of credentials is what qualified me

I usually do not argue with God because it is a waste of time. This time I did. "God, how are you going to use me to do this? I am not qualified." And that is when God answered my prayer. I realized I was exactly perfectly qualified. My extreme lack of credentials is what qualified me to be a miracle with God's help.

> *"I can do all things through Christ which strengtheneth me." Philippians 4:13 KJV*

Chapter 17

Commodore 64 Robotics

While in the hospital I started working to build robotics systems using a Commodore 64 and then the Commodore 128. There was a Commodore users' group that met in one of the meeting rooms of the hospital, so I was able to get started with help. I purchased parts from Radio shack and started to build. The first time I connected my circuit board to the Commodore it blew up with smoke and sparks everywhere.

I upgraded to the Commodore 128 and built a "buffer box" to go between the Computer and my projects. The user group was able to help me with the programming, but I had very little help on the circuit boards. Most of them failed to work properly, at least the "buffer box" prevented me from blowing any more computers.

We did not have the internet back then so getting information was slow. Imagine trying to build a robot suit without the help of the internet. I wrote some letters to professors at Berkeley, the University of Washington, and a few others. Only a couple of people wrote me back. I did actually get better responses from the department of the Army research labs when I mentioned that I believed that the LIFESUIT could be used by paratroopers to prevent injuries like the one I had experienced that put me in the hospital in the first place.

I had for many years purchased experiment instructions and weird science kits from the back of Popular Science magazine and even some comic books.

One of the experiments I was working on as a teenager used a broken television as a high voltage power supply (very dangerous by the way, don't try this at home). I believed I could build Ion Ram Jet Engines that would be powerful enough to lift a hover car. I dreamed of powering them with hydrogen fuel. I wanted to use a new type of internal combustion engine I was going to invent. After splitting salt water with electricity into hydrogen and oxygen I realized I had the raw material I needed.

For a new light weight material imagined if I could inject a lot of air into some ceramic similar to the bubbles in shaving cream the majority of the volume of such a ceramic would be air. I believed this would be strong and able to handle high temperature. After playing with soap and clay I was able to get some extra volume but whenever I fired the clay the bubbles popped, and the structure fell apart.

It was this sort of visioning and experimentation that gave me a little practical experience to believe I could make the LIFESSUIT a reality.

I realized what I needed to make the LIFESUIT robotic exoskeleton a reality was to find other mad scientists that were willing to work with me to make science fiction real.

Later in 2000, I met Doug Bell who introduced me to Bill Beaty who ran the weird science club called the weird science salon. http://amasci.com/weird.html This club meets the first Friday of the month to share ideas about developing new and weird science. I met a lot of scientists at this club.

I just needed to Get STARTED-don't quit.

Chapter 18

Have a Pity Party

Being in the hospital was the lowest of the low points for me in my life. Prior to that I was on top of the world and invincible. I thought I would live forever. Everything I touched turned to gold and I got 100% scores on all of my tests.

"The future was so dark I felt blind"…..

Then it hit me: I was an invalid. An … In Valid… No value to society. NO benefit…. Only a drag on family, friends, community, society. I was a nothing a nobody and I was told I could not go to school and I would never walk again.

The future was so dark I felt blind…..

To add insult to injury, I had fallen from over 100 feet to break my back and did not die. The hospital only had eight floors and if I could somehow get to the roof and throw myself off that was only eighty feet and if one hundred feet would not kill me, well eight surely would not be enough. It was hopeless.

Well as Dave Lister, would say "Even the word hopeless had the word hope in it."

The only thing I had to look forward to, was the highlight of my day at dinner time: Included with the evening meal was a photocopied sheet of paper with the next day's menu on it. I could check the boxes of the foods I would like to try for the next three meals. This was an extension of my foodie experience. It was hospital food After all. I did explore the full menu and whenever there was something I had not tried, I checked it off by circling it and the next day that was what I had.

Get STARTED-don't quit!

Being an army hospital, the nurses were not trained to be especially helpful to paralyzed patients. I do not know why it was but when I had to eat there was no one to help me shovel the food into my mouth. Frequently, the dinner tray was over my head and I would reach up with my fingers and try to determine what the food was. I would grab some and drop it into my mouth. Many times, the food got in my eyes and up my nose. This led to me choosing items on the menu that could be sandwich foods.

For breakfast I had scrambled or hard-boiled eggs with toast that I could wrap into a sandwich. I got really good at making the sandwich on the tray over my head without seeing what was on the plate. I learned to see with my hands. I quickly decided to not have soups or stews; these were the worst when eating in this fashion.

Today I know the nurses and hospital staff is there for the soldiers and when they are in my situation, they have someone who will feed them. For that I am thankful. For me, back then, it was humiliating to dump food in my face while I was eating, when I could not even walk.

I found I was so depressed everyday it was hard to focus on the future. I was thinking about suicide daily and even sometimes, minute by minute.

This is a warning to anyone who has a family member who has recently been paralyzed. There is a group on the planet that sells themselves as humanitarian and nonprofit, who are there to support the dignity of the sick and lame. They are the Hemlock society and they worship the gods like Kevorkian.

They prey on the paralyzed and their families. In the internal memos they teach their activists to comb the news looking for people who have been paralyzed and get to them within the first few months because they know that paralyzed people are the most depressed during the first six months. They know if they can get to

81

them within the first two months, they can almost always get them to commit assisted suicide. A victory for them, a victory for Kevorkian and a victory for Satan.

Ninety five percent of paralyzed people who get through the first six months decide to survive and they do very well. Most of them become over achievers.

I realized it was too much for me to be upset all of the time. It was draining and painful just to be alive with all of the negative thoughts.

My new friend Lyn O'Neal, a business consultant and professor of business at the Monterey Peninsula College gave me a copy of Denis Waitley's "Seeds of Greatness" in audio format. I listened to that program over and over. I determined I would live life and live it more abundantly. With this new determination I had to do something to get away from the daily focus on the negative.

I decided to schedule my pain, suffering, ranting and raving. Whenever I took a breath and it was too painful to think I would get out my schedule and turn to Thursday at two pm. In that appointment details section on my calendar I would write the thing I was upset about. By writing it down I was able to let it go a little. Then on Thursday at two pm I would open the schedule and read all of the things I was upset about over the last week and vent on it. I would think, reflect, yell and scream. Sometimes I would put my pillow over my face and pull hard while yelling at the top of my lungs. Later I was able to bring this forward and do a workout during that time and beat on the punching bag while I was venting. Even later still I was able to run during that pity party and vent off all of the negative energy.

If you have never done this, I recommend you try it. You will be amazed at the results.

Later I started to use the Franklin planner. In that time management system, I would make a daily list and determine priorities. In the back of the book I kept numbered tabs for projects. One of those numbered tabs is my Thursday two pm pity party.

Schedule your own Pity Party. Pick a day and time that will allow you one hour to process all of the junk from the week before. This is very useful. It works better if you can do this with a workout of some kind. When I used the punching bag or the treadmill, I was able to burn a lot of calories and frustration at the same time.

Get a pocket notebook or a handful of three by five cards (3x5 inch notecards) and keep them with you everywhere you go. Whenever you have a negative thought you will want to take out the pocket notebook or the 3x5's and write down the topic of frustration. Write the name of the frustration point, record what was said or done to make you think of it. Write down the words that popped into you head. I am serious, think about what horrible things you said to yourself and write it down. Think about physiological symptoms. What was your skin temperature? Did your temperature go up or down? Did you experience perspiration? Or a cold clammy feeling? Did you feel your heartbeat increase? Was your pulse so strong you felt throbbing in your forehead or throat? Did a headache come on? Do a checkup from the neck up and record all of the self-talk that was related to this negative incident. Assess all of your body sensations.

Some people notice that they have manifestations of smells that are not there, but they sense them during a negative incident. Many memories that have negative effect hold onto you and keep haunting you.

Cognitive Behavior Therapy is a way to proactively cause positive effects in your life. When you are done venting and reflecting on all of the negative you will process the trauma of the week. Then you want to come up with positive self-talk and mantras that will help program your mind to be better.

Your subconscious does not know the difference between a memory or an imagination. So, you can write your imaginations in a way that program your subconscious to seek out success and wellbeing.

Instead of saying how much this "F***ing sucks" I would rewrite a comment "This is amazing that I am alive today, I can breathe clean air and think straight" I would even go so far as to create statements prophetically speaking over my life. "Every cell in my spine has been healed, the bones have restructured and healed, the nerves share no pain only bliss with my mind."

"Every day in every way I am feeling better and better"

"Every night I sleep well, and wake refreshed"

"I have supernatural energy every time I wake"

"My mind absorbs knowledge and retains all"

Chapter 19

Master Mind Problem Solving

What if you could have Albert Einstein at your next problem-solving meeting?

Figure 11 Albert Einstein with Monty Reed (actually it is my friend Dane Lindsay who I met in Israel. He has been accused of looking like Albert. Photo taken in Tel Aviv at the airport.)

In the hospital, I developed a near insatiable hunger for biographies of successful people. Based on my understanding of who they were from the biographies I have read; I have an imagined avatar of who they are and how they would react in one of my brainstorming meetings. This is NOT "woo woo" or any kind of spiritual thing and it is NOT calling up the ghosts. This is an exercise in my own imagination.

I pretend or make believe they are alive and well and participating in my meetings. If I need to promote a public event, I imagine a great magician and some rock

85

stars are at the table helping me come up with a way to promote the event.

Figure 12 Monty Reed with Rock Star Joan Jett

Sometimes it is just me in the room with my eyes closed and around the table are seven to twelve famous imaginary people from history to help me solve a problem. I imagine Albert Einstein playing a practical joke on Abraham Lincoln while Pythagoras of Samos is cracking a joke about polygons to Joan Jett.

I read about: Benjamin Franklin, Abraham Lincoln, Andre Meyer, John F. Kennedy, Winston Churchill, Theodore Roosevelt, George Washington, Erich Weise (aka Harry Houdini), Harry Blackstone, Socrates,

Michael Faraday, Alan Mulally, Galileo Galilei, Leonardo Da Vinci and a few you may have never heard of. Several Average Joe types as well.

Figure 13 Monty Reed with Alan Mulally Ford CEO and President

The master mind problem solving technique can work in two ways.

The easiest way is to find a tribe of people who have similar beliefs to your own and ask them to meet with you on a regular basis. Usually a weekly meeting for nintey days is a great way to get started. Have a specific goal in mind, like, you want your business to grow five times in sales annually, and get together weekly to do some brainstorming. I recommend you pray for each others needs as well as work on coming up with solutions for each others challenges.

When I was in the hospital I found other patients who wanted to recover from the ailment they had and started to mastermind on what we would do when we got out of the hospital and were no longer plagued with our illness.

Figure 14 Monty Reed with Chuck Girard formerly of the band Love Song

Many years later when I purchased a seventy five acre horse property in Monroe Washington, I found other horse barn owners that I liked and started to meet with them once a month for breakfast. Even though we were competitors we had things in common that we needed and when we worked together we had buying power for things like feed, hay and shavings for the barn. We also taked a bit about web sites and advertising too. When I first called the competing barns to meet up they were a bit reluctant to meet with me. They did not want to give away secrets. I told them I was planning on being full and needed to have a barn I knew was amazing that I could refer clients to when we were full. Because I was so positive about my business plan they agreed to meet with me on a regular basis. From this pool of people, I found a couple of new friends too.

The other way to mastermind is using your imagination to bring together an imaginary group for a mastermind meeting. This can be a group of dead people from history or people that are still alive. This is the one I use the most. You need to have a knowledge of the other peoples lives, by having read biographies or knowing them personally. You have to use your imagination to get them to contribute. Try it. You have nothing to lose and everything to gain.

Figure 15 Monty Reed, John Schlitt formerly of Petra, Marianne McGuire, Darrin Pederson and Rodney from the band "Storm Warrior" who opened the show for John. This is the band Monty was in for a few years.

Figure 16 Les Neu, Monty Reed and Senator Patty Murray

I have interviewed millionaires, politicians and rock stars that I have admired. When I can I buy them a drink or a meal to spend time with them. Millionaires really like it when you buy them lunch, billionaires like it even more. Everyone is always trying to get a free lunch out of them

89

so when you offer to buy them lunch, they usually really appreciate it.

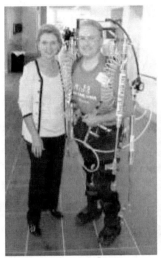

Figure 17 former Governor Gregoir and Monty Reed

Figure 18 Monty, Representative Jim McDermott and Dr Stiens

Most politicians will meet with you if it makes them look good. Some of them actually do take steps to help you with your cause. Christine, Patty and Jim all told me they would make sure we got funding, and nothing ever came from any efforts or connections they had. I did show up for functions with them and it did make them look good. All of their supporters have also supported my work verbally too. It seemed like a great match and we waited for the promised funding. There are other politicians that are all do and no talk.

Mayor Charles Royer was the first sponsor of They Shall Walk when he awarded me a scholarship for my pioneering work in Robotics back in 1987.

90

Figure 19 Mayor Charles Royer presenting to Monty Reed the Mayors Small Business Scholarship. Photo by Mark Reed

I saw the posting for the small business scholarship at the college financial aid office. Back in 1987 the scholarships were photo copies in a binder. There was no real internet to speak of yet. I mean it was there but not very useful yet. I called the office of the Mayor and the woman at the desk told me if I got the application to her office by 3pm it would be added to the applications. It was just after noon. I figured I had about an hour to write and print the application and the essay and then I needed to jet to the downtown office.

I made it and, in a few days, got the call that I was awarded one of two small business scholarships. This photo was taken by my brother Mark at the award dinner where I received the scholarship and the check.

Figure 20 They Shall Walk Lab Crew with Mayor Mike McGinn (3rd from the right)

More recently Mayor Mike McGinn supported They Shall Walk research by featuring us in his neighborhood walks. He also invited me to sit on the committee for disAbilities at the city of Seattle.

Mike invited me to several of his private dinner events and introduced me to many of his supporters who became financial supporters of They Shall Walk. He was very helpful during the years when donations were light, because the people he introduced me to actually helped support us financially. After all you cannot pay the power bill with handshakes and hugs.

Chapter 20

Coming Home

I finally knew I would be going home soon. Orders in hand I
made a phone call to the Seattle Veterans Administration
Medical Center (VAMC). After a few minutes I had a live
person on the phone. I explained that I wanted to make an
appointment to see a physical therapist or a doctor to give me
a referral to a physical therapist so I could continue my daily
physical therapy (PT). The person started to ask for my
name, address and a few other things when my ID number
did not come up in the system.

"What Veterans hospital are you at right now?" she asked. I
explained that I was in an Army hospital and I wanted to
schedule PT so I could continue my daily therapy as soon as
I moved back to Seattle.

"You are not at a Veterans hospital now?" she asked with an
obviously irritated tone. "No, it is an Army hospital" I
answered back. "You are not a Veteran?" she asked, even
more irritated. "No, I am active duty with orders to get out
and become a Veteran in a couple months." She tried to
interrupt me, but I made my point. It did not matter what I
was trying to do, all that mattered to her was that I was not a
Veteran and so she did not have to talk to me, and she could
not help me. "Call back after you are discharged and then
we can schedule you for your appointment."

I was so sad and angry all at once. I just wanted reasonable
care; I wanted my daily PT routine to continue un-interrupted.
This system was broken and there was nothing I could do
about it. I did call as soon as I was a Veteran as I was
getting ready to leave Fort Ord, I called the Seattle VAMC to
see if I could schedule the appointment. They told me I

93

would get on a list and they would call me when they had an opening.

One year later almost to the date, the phone rang, and it was the Seattle VAMC with an opening. The broken VA medical system had wrecked my therapy routine. That year was horrible. Every spare penny I could scrape together I used to buy another physical therapy session.

When I got out of the Army, I was told during our briefing that I had earned a special six months of unemployment that could help me get back on my feet. When I filled the paperwork, they told me I was not eligible because I could not work. When I applied for disability with the State, I was told I was ineligible for State disability because I was injured in Germany and not in the State of Washington. If I had lied and said I was injured on Fort Lewis I would have been eligible. I told the truth and was denied.

My father loved me and gave me my old room back. I could not do much for him because I could only sit or stand for fifteen minutes at a time and then I needed to lay down. I was able to cook dinners for him and he did not even expect that.

"I just wanted my country to love me as much as I loved it."

I was very sad about the way my country treated me after I had risked my life to protect it, I had lost my old life because of my disabilities. "I just wanted my country to love me as much as I loved it."

In addition to the pain and problems walking, I suffered from nightmares that made it very difficult to sleep. If it was not a nightmare waking me, it was the pain. Some nights I would wake up because it hurt too much to breath. Gasping for air I would take some more pain medicine and sleeping pills and go back to sleep.

Percocet during the day, Valium and sleeping pills at night... Most days all I wanted to do was go back to sleep because it hurt so bad.

Chapter 21

Overcoming Learning DisAbilities

As a child my grandmother trained my siblings and I to paint and sculpt, she also felt it was her responsibility to get me exposed to theater and the arts. It stuck, I love art and artists, art allows us to experience more of life. I had painted a little when I was in the hospital and wanted to see if I could learn to do any amazing art.

At the North Seattle Community College, (now NorthSeattle.edu) I wanted to just register to take some art classes since I had been told I could not go to college when I was in high school. I was told that I still had to take the college entrance tests. I suggested that I pay for the tests and we just save a little time and put an F on the math and English, so I do not have to take them. The testing administrator said that would not fly. She asked me to take the math test and use scratch paper. "Bring the scratch paper back and turn it in with your test so we can analyze it.

After taking the tests the woman who worked in the testing office showed me the simple obvious mistakes I had made in the math. I had flipped numbers around, treated division symbols as if they were minus and addition symbols as if they were multiplications and negative numbers were treated as positives.

After less than a minute she asked if I was willing to take a few more tests at no charge. She said the scratch paper indicated that I may have a learning disAbility and the tests may help identify some tools that will help me learn.

After three hours the test was scored by a machine and we had some results. I had a learning disAbility and if I were to do four things different, I would be able to enroll into college.

96

I registered for a full load and began. With the new tools I was able to get on the dean's list in my second quarter and became the president of the honors society. The Alpha Epsilon Omega Chapter of Phi Theta Kappa. I went to the national convention and met an amazing young lady, Danshera Wetherington. She became the love of my life.

I had courted many women up until this point and she was the first one who I had become engaged to. We were so opposite in many ways that we really were the example of iron sharpening iron. After a year, things did not work out and we moved on. We have been able to stay friends through it all. I consider myself a better person for having met her.

Everyone has different tools they need to access in order to learn when they are differently-abled. If you are having challenges with your studies go to the school counseling office, ask your parents and your teachers for help and testing.

I had to take some time off from college because of health issues.

Chapter 22

The Convenience Store and Network Marketing

When I first got out of the hospital in July of 1987, my father let me have my old room back. I was able to stay with my father for a few months. No one would even interview me for a job when I told them that I could not sit or stand longer than fifteen minutes. There was not ADA (Americans with Disabilities Act) until 1990 and this was 1987.

The father of a friend of mine from high school, Roger Francis, had a convenience store. When I mentioned I was looking for work he told me he would rather play golf than count the money and do the books. If I needed to lay on the floor, I could use his dog's pillow in the office. After one training session he went to go play golf. He told me "Don't call me, do not interrupt my golf game, you can figure it out, I will see you tomorrow." I was the assistant manager and worked two to three days a week for a year and a half.

One thing about convenience stores is the high turnover of the employees. One day I was laying on the floor counting the money and doing the books. The money was spread all around the office floor because I was counting it. One of the new employees came into the office unannounced to get high valued items to restock the floor.

When he opened the door and saw me laying on the floor with money spread out all around the office floor he yelled. "What happened?! are you okay?" When I tried to calm him down, I said "it is okay, I just broke my back" he really lost it. I tried to explain to him that it was a year and a half before, but it was too late. He quit.

A year and a half after starting that job I had an appointment with the owner and told him that my business was doing well

98

and I needed to quit working for him so I could focus on my own business. His response was "That is what we all hope for." He thanked me and let me go be about my business.

The same month I started my job at 7-Eleven, I started my own business and began to look for health insurance for my employees that I would one day soon be hiring. I expected my business to grow and so I knew I wanted to have the best benefits for my employees. I was going to take real good care of my people. I went to a small business event and met Joe Voutour, who was selling insurance and investments. I scheduled an appointment with him at my place of business in my dads' home.

Joe came over and we started talking about dreams and goals. Joe was one of those people I would choose to have in my tribe. What I mean by that is, there are people out there that have similar values and goals to your core beliefs and those are the people you would choose if you were putting together a tribe of people. Joe talked about; patriotism, God first, Country second, Family third, Career fourth and everything else after that. I loved it and adopted these terms to explain the way I already feel about values.

One of the nicest things about these priorities is that it makes it so easy to make snap decisions when you are under pressure. For instance: the child has a school event and the job has a meeting or expo that needs to be covered…. What do you do? Simple… Family comes before Career, so you decide to spend the time with the child's school event. If your values are different you will make your decisions in another way. I recommend you determine what your values are and run some tests on situations to see how you would really decide. Then once you have determined your values you write them down and stick to your guns.

Joe said, "Since you are open to other ways of making money, I would like to show you a project I am working in with a few people every year." This sounded interesting and of course I agreed.

He started drawing these circles in what I later found out was called STP (Showing The Plan). I had seen that somewhere, a few years before when I had been visiting my friend Ryan Hill and Janeen Bloss, (another love of my life from high the high school years). This guy had drawn circles and talked about a network of entrepreneurs that could span the globe if we just got enough people involved. When I had seen these circles, I was active duty in the commando unit, and we were going after world peace by force.

I realized at this pinnacle moment in my life, if we could get enough people into this network marketing thing, we could have world peace without force. This could work so much better than the peace by force program we were under way with already.

I looked at Joe and said "This is that… that. that thing, with the circles… ah…." I was so excited, and Joe had no idea what I was thinking. I grabbed his brief case and threw it open. I started digging through the papers in his case until I saw it… The logo and the company name I was looking for "Amway."

"This is Amway, isn't it?" Joe's mouth dropped open and he inhaled in a gasp. "What do you know about it?" he asked with a defensive smile. "Get me one of those kits, I've been looking for someone to sign me up for over two years." The next day, I met Joe and his wife Shirley at a Jack in the box on Westlake in downtown Seattle to buy my starter kit for the Amway business.

Over the next thirty years I worked in a number of network marketing businesses and was very successful in Nikken as a Platinum and Thrive Life as a Diamond in Training.

"Five years from now you will be exactly the same except for: the books you read, the audios you listen to and the people you associate with." Is one of my favorite anonymous quotes. I began going to seminars, reading books and listening to audio recordings. At those seminars I met a lot of like-minded people.

More people for my tribe. I met Steve and Jenne. We hit it off right quick. I loved those two from the moment I met them. She was brilliant and always seemed happy. He was a handsome young firefighter that had everything going for him and he had started his own network marketing business. Steve and I were inseparable. We were going to take on the world and live our dreams. We would go to these meetings at the museum of history and industry and then go out for pie after and talk about becoming millionaires with the freedom to invent things.

I had never met anyone who had as many ideas for inventions as I did. He had this firefighting grenade idea that I thought could change the world all by itself. Because I had experience with demolitions and hand grenades, we worked together on making this thing a reality.

The fact that he had never gone in the military did not matter because his work in the fire service was very much like that of a soldier's life. We had a comradery that went beyond a simple friendship. We were best friends.
I had a chance to watch his kids when he and his wife needed a time out. I remember Nick was at my house one time and my roommate asked "What's he doing here" I said I was babysitting, and Nick was very quick to correct me.

"Kid sitting, you are kid sitting, not babysitting. I'm not a baby." All of their kids were smart.

We did a lot of double date, and group date events with them too. Mostly other like-minded people. Entrepreneurs who believed in the American way, free enterprise and the values we had for family.

Lizzy is like another daughter to me. I still have friends who think I had two daughters because Lizzy would spend the night with us on weekends and go with us to church.

Figure 21 The Reed Family: Stacy, Monty, Ciara and Isaac

Chapter 23

Royal Knights Security

I was approached by two guys in trench coats, I remember thinking "this is so cliché." When they started asking me questions it was clear they knew a lot about me. They knew my whole 'jacket' from my Army Ranger days, even the classified stuff. These were the first "Independent Contractors" I had met since I was out of the Army.

I had been doing my physical therapy and moved onto the gym to regain my strength. I still had chronic pain every day, but I was able to get around more and do more.

I took some contract work doing security. Most of it was guarding houses, buildings, vehicles in transit with clients on board. At first it was just a few things here and there, then there was more than I could handle myself and I hired some military buddies who could handle the job. For soldiers who had been in it, this sort of work came easy. Rangers were always my choice because the SOP (Standard Operating Procedure) was so familiar that I would not have to train them as much, just plug and play security. When I work with other Rangers it is like working with an extension of my own body. I literally do not have to speak to them. We work together as if we are reading each other's minds.

"Too Live Crew" the band, was coming to Seattle and the show promoters came to me because a memo had gone out that no Seattle Police Department officers were allowed to work off duty security for this event and the SPD would not come any closer to the Paramount theater than across the street. The promoters wanted me to arrange security because a lot of the people who were going to attend the show were from the Crips and the Bloods street gangs (aka clubs). The promoters wanted to allow them both to attend the show, enjoy it and not have any fighting.

I had to pray about accepting that job because it seemed impossible to keep that environment secure without any shooting going on. After some time in prayer and the promoters increasing my fee, I met with them to work out the logistics. From what I could tell from the "word on the street" was that there was no way the intended attendees would show up without "packing" (they were all going to be armed). I went a little old school on them with the "fight fire with fire" approach. I told the promoters I would need freedom to pull security the way I wanted to. They gave me that freedom.

In order for a person to be hired to pull security during that concert they had to have a concealed weapons permit (CWP) and be willing to carry a full kit of concealed gear. The kit included: cuffs, tear gas, collapsing baton, zip ties, semi-automatic pistol, carbine or shotgun.

Everything in the kit had to be concealed in holsters, bags, pockets or under a coat. We all dressed in black and wore t-shirts or jackets with two-inch white lettering that said: Guns, Ammunition and Police Supplies. We all patrolled the venue in two and three-man teams. I remember seeing the leadership of the gangs take up turf inside the Paramount Theater. Every one of them were dressed in bulky long jackets that had lots of bulges.

At the end of the night there were only a couple of scuffles with some non-gang members who tried to start something with us, it was the gang members that stepped in between us and the unruly ones and straightened them out.

We had one incident when somebody was threatening one of the gang members, reinforcements were starting to pile into the hallway and when five of our guys walked into the middle of the conflict with obvious bulges the fight dispersed.

I never found out just how much firepower they were packing, because we did our job, we respected them, and they respected us. We knew they were packing, and they knew we were too. I believe God sent angels to watch over me and my crew while we watched over the crowd and the band "Too Live Crew."

We continued to do security jobs actively for few years. We did not need to advertise since satisfied clients referred us to other happy customers. The money was good, and there were risks that went with the funds.

I enjoyed the security work however I must say my favorite vocation is public speaking and consulting. I solved problems for people. My favorite clients call me Mr. Solution. I was getting paid $150 a day in 1990. In 1996 a client offered me $1750 a day for a six-month contract because he liked the way I was delivering a talk one evening. The current rate is $5000 a day and I prefer to travel one week a month doing six cities in six days. That way I have the other three weeks for family and friends.

For schools, churches and charities my fees are negotiable, and I will usually make an appearance in exchange for an offering of some kind.

Chapter 24

Mountain Castle

Monty means "royalty of the mountain castle." When I looked at my background and my abilities, I knew sporting goods. Since I could only do part time work and had to spend a lot of time laying on the floor because of my back I had an Entrepreneurial Seizure. I started a sporting goods store.

At first it was in my father's basement under the stairs. I got the license and started making contacts with suppliers. I booked a table at sporting show and invested about five hundred dollars into business cards, fliers and price tags. I borrowed sporting goods from everyone I knew and looked up the prices for those items. On the price tags I put the NEW price and the USED price.

I had to imagine I had a retail store and that I would buy and sell new and used items. Then I estimated what my used prices would be. I priced all of my items and then added some big red tags (two by five inches) that had the word SOLD on them.

To be a visionary is one thing but to make something happen you have to act.

"Faith without works is dead"
James 2:20 KJV

When I was at the sportsman's show there were thousands of people and hundreds of vendors. I took over a thousand dollars in orders for merchandise that day. First thing on Monday I placed orders and called the customers to let them know when their items should be in. I asked everyone for referrals and pretty soon the business was booming. The first year I grossed a little over $20,000. The second year I brought

106

in over $100,000 and the third year my gross was half a million. I had hired an assistant manager who was like a brother to me. He ran the store and hired sales people for my so I could focus on marketing and expanding my business.

This was no accident because I had placed the "5X" symbol everywhere. It was on my mirror in the house, on the cash register facing myself and the sales reps, it was on the back of the display cases, it was written on my day planner on every page. It meant to grow the business sales by five times. That is exactly what we did.

We added wholesale and mail order to the cash-flow. In addition to the retail store we did sportsman's shows a few times a month.

I met a variety of people by having the retail store. A lot of my friends were in law enforcement, so I took an interest in police supplies. Some of my customers were Seattle Police, King and Snohomish County deputies, Federal Marshals, DEA, FBI and some independent contractors that worked for the Fed's.

My accountant called me into my office where he had been going over the books. "There is thirty-six thousand dollars missing from this month" he told me with a stern look on his face. I countered "you mean thirty-six hundred, right?" He shook his head no. "I have been going over it again and again. The books have been cooked and it is pretty ingenious how well it was done." He continued "if this was not so disturbing, I would be impressed." He explained to me that it was most likely that the COD shipments were being paid for with cash out of the register and then there was a large number of transactions that were not recorded.

We had a problem; well I had a problem. A guy who I thought was my friend was stealing from me and only hiring people who would steal from me. I had to fire everyone, hire a new manager and find out just how bad it was. It was not just the house keeping aspect of getting the business stable it was the painful stab in the back from the store manager that had been stealing from me all while smiling and looking me in the eye every day.

After calling all my suppliers and doing a little investigation I found that several firearms had been shipped to me that had not been recorded in my log book. The manager and his crew were stealing money and firearms. In the midst of the investigation I heard the previous manager was planning on hurting himself after hurting his entire family.

When I realized that firearms were stolen from me, I did what I thought was the right thing to do. I called the Seattle Police, FBI, and the BATF (Bureau of Alcohol Tobacco and Firearms) to report it. The SPD and the FBI were very helpful and seemed concerned with finding out the truth.

The ATF agent kept stalling and would not give me any strait answers. He seemed too busy to take my calls or return my calls. I found out later that he had granted immunity to my ex manager if he would testify against me.

The ATF agent was a crook. He was planning on making an example of me and using this case to build his career and get a promotion. Because of his greed and lust for power he was ignorant to the facts and did not care about the truth.

I could not believe this was happening. Several people came out of the wood-work to tell me this guy was a bad cop and that he was building a strong case with professional witnesses that would say anything he told them to. Several of the guys who had been working for me and stealing from me came to me to say they were sorry and that they also were going to testify against me to protect themselves. One guy came and told me "they were watching and had witnesses that would lie about

108

me so they will win the case." He also said he was leaving town, so he did not have to be one of those fake witnesses.

This situation seemed worse than I could have imagined it could be. After all I had been through, how could this be happening to me? I hired a lawyer who told me I could be going to jail for one hundred and fifty years and paying a fine of over a hundred thousand dollars. The one hundred and fifty years was not an understatement. This was the minimum mandatory sentence for me as the federally licenses firearms dealer. Five years for every occurrence of a gun not recorded in the book as it came into the store and another five for when it went out. Since the thieves were not recording the guns they ordered and stole from me, I was on the hook for ten years each, for fifteen firearms that I had found in my investigation. I felt even worse for my wife because she had just come into my life.

I prayed a lot while I waited for the court date. I had a vision that I was going to go to jail for decades and in the vision, I decided the prison would be my bible college. In the vision I became a bible scholar in jail.

"I saw a dream which made me afraid, and the thoughts upon my bed and the visions of my head troubled me." Daniel 4:5 KJV

Lucky for me I did not believe in predestination. God has shown me that his visions have been used as a warning: not of what *is* to come but of what *could* come. I prayed for God to deliver me and I prayed most of all for the TRUTH.

"know the truth, and the truth shall make you free." John 8:32 KJV

A series of "death in the family" for the prosecutor, the judge and somebody else involved in my case delayed the court date two times so it was now eighteen months after the original date. The day before court a letter came in the mail from the BATF. It was a copy of a copy of a copy that was hard to read. It was instructing me to ship all my records to the Federal records repository because my license had expired. I put them all in a box and shipped them "overnight" with guaranteed delivery first thing in the morning.

The next morning just outside of the court room the bad cop approached. "You got my records?" he asked with an evil grin. When I told him, I had already shipped them to the ATF records depository he blew a gasket as he ripped the shipping bill from my hand and ran down the hall to use the payphone. He was yelling at the shipper "I don't care if you have already delivered it you get that box back on the truck and ship it back here now!"

Just as he stormed back into the waiting area we were called into the courtroom.

I prayed for favor before the magistrates.

"...when they bring you... unto magistrates... take ye no thought how or what thing ye shall answer, or what ye shall say" Luke 12:11 KJV

The judge had heard all the evidence and asked if I had anything to say for myself or to the court.

I expressed to the judge that I was very sorry that this happened. I should have been more responsible; my name was on the license and because of that I take full responsibility for the consequences. "I am trusting God and I throw myself on the mercy of the court and you, your honor."

The Judge looked at his notes as I prayed. It seemed
like hours even though it was probably only ten minutes.

The Judge read some stuff from his notes and exclaimed
"$100 fine and one-year probation." The gavel slammed as
the bad cop yelled at the Judge. "Order, order in my
courtroom!" the judge was repeating as the gavel slammed
over and over. My attorney escorted me out and to the fine
booth where I paid my fine.

I was terrified that I would have one of those bad probation
officers you see in a low budget movie that was mean and
would take advantage of me. I prayed and gave over my
worry to God.

When the probation officer showed up, she was the most
beautiful blonde I had seen in years. She could have been a
model. She had long legs, a beautiful figure, an amazing
smile. My wife and I told her she could come anytime she
wanted for those surprise inspections and monthly meetings.

God sure has a sense of humor and cares about all of
the little things. To think that my fear of a greasy, slimy
probation officer would be met by God sending an officer
that was a ten in the beauty department just because
God cared. He did not have to do that for me. It was
enough that he spared me the one hundred and fifty
years of prison. God going the extra mile was just so I
would know he was real. You gotta love it.

Chapter 25

My Other Best Friend

After getting out of the Army with a broken back, job prospects were not so good. The ADA (Americans with Disabilities Act) would not come out until 1990. I found part time work for the couple of hours a week I was able to work and thought about what skills I could use to start my own business. One thing I was very familiar with was the weapons of the world. I could disassemble a Colt 1911A 45 caliber pistol in seven seconds blindfolded and put it back together in eleven seconds.

A lot of soldiers get out of the military and go straight into the most dangerous job they can find: police, firefighter, high rise construction and private security. Because of my back injury I did not have that option. So, I started my own business in the sporting goods industry. I opened a retail sporting goods store with an emphasis on firearms. In addition to the retail sporting goods store I also worked gun shows on the weekend. This helped promote my store and grow my business. I also was able to see the latest and greatest inventory that was out there.

Some shows we did well at and others it was more like a community service to be there. Two months before, I had just been analyzing my sales and expenses and decided that I would never do the Everett Washington Gun show again because the expenses and the sales did not make it worth it, ever.

I told my employees "We are not doing that gun show in Everett, ever. If I ever tell you we are doing that gun show, remind me of what I have said here." I even went so far as to tell them if they let me do that gun show they would be fired.

112

Get STARTED-don't quit!

Two months after I had given them this little speech, I woke up early on a Saturday and called the staff together to let them know we were doing the Everett gun show. They were like "boss, you said….."   I shooshed them and said "I know, I know…. I just have a feeling about this show, and we have to do it." They grumbled a bit and reluctantly went along with it. After all I was the boss, this was not a democracy. They did not get commissions; they did have profit sharing though and so the profitability of the business was in their best interest.

I was at this gun show, selling guns and from the other side of the room I heard a shout out "Hey you!" When I looked over, I saw the most beautiful creature I had ever laid my eyes on, a real beauty. I made a bee line for her. She was sitting on a table and when I got to her I sat on the table next to her and looked into her eyes and said "So, when are we going dancing?"

Two days later, on Monday, we had our first date. We had lunch, took a walk, went to dinner and dancing. A couple of days later she had an engagement ring. A year later we were married and have been together ever since.

The first few years we had all the same issues that most newlyweds do. The difference is that we just decided to 'stay married'. You know, "till death do you part" and all that. She is my other best friend, my wife, my love, my life. Together we have shared business, family and friends.

She was the last in a family of nine and I was the middle of three children. The family reunions took a few years for me to get used to and of course now I fully enjoy having such a large family.

We just celebrated 29 years together by touring the holy land with our friends.

Figure 22 Stacy Reed and Monty Reed at the City of David dig in Israel

Figure 23 Stacy and Monty Reed under the old city of Jerusalem in the Jewish quarter

Chapter 26
Number One

As Newlyweds we adopted a teenager. I tell people, tongue in cheek, that this almost prevented us from ever having children. However, it prepared us to be better parents.

My Number One. Tony was my first son; my first child and I love him more than I can say. I fell in love with Tony when he was eight and still very cute. When his mom was diagnosed with cancer he started to act up. It was a text book case of abandonment syndrome, he was mad at his mother for leaving even though she was still with us. I was a newlywed, so I approached my wife first to talk about adoption.

Tony was my step nephew in law. His mother had him before she met her husband whose mother was my father's second wife (Tony's grandmother was my step mother).

When Tony started acting up, no-one wanted him but his mother. I got a phone call from Tony and he told me his step father had been knocking him around. I told him I was on my way. When I got to his house, I told his father Tony would be living with us for a while. Tony moved in with me that night.

I met with his mother and we wrote up some papers so that I could adopt Tony. We did not have any money to pay the attorneys to make it legal but that does not matter to me. Tony is my number one son and that is why my nick name for him is "Number One."

He has made us proud grandparents and we are excited to spend more time with our extended family.

Chapter 27

Starting Over

What a ride it was from there in 1990. After closing the store, we were $256,000 in debt. We filed a chapter 13 bankruptcy so we could "Work instead of sleep until it was all paid back." We had one car that sort of worked and we did what we could taking part time jobs. Every month we met with the court appointed accountant to hand over our garage sale money and paychecks. The would let us keep a little and then dole out the rest to creditors.

My wife just enrolled in a training program to get a certificate in administration. I took a telemarketing job in the same building.

In this job your position in the room was based on your sales performance. When you were brand-new you started on the back row. The company had over thirty people who worked there. If you were number one you sat in the front row on the left. If you are last in sales, you sat in the back row on the far right. After my first week I noticed I could go through the script without even really thinking about it. By the second week I noticed I could do the script and think about other things.

"Hello this is Monty Reed from the Seattle Times at 2nd and John Street... blah blah blah etc."

I brought my Bible to work and noticed that I could read the Bible while reciting the script and making sales.

Every day, every week, I was number two in sales or number one. I never dropped down to number three in sales.

I had only been there for a few weeks and the manager was loving me. At the first coffee break one day he called me into his office and closed the door. He said after taking a big deep breath and a sigh "You know there's someone complaining that you have to Bible here at work. I can't tell you who it is, but you know who it is. I will tell you what I told him. I told him, to come back and talk to me after he gets to the front row." He cleared his throat and continued. "So, Monty, do us both a favor and stay in that top position. And help your friends to stay in their top positions too. So, I'm not going to tell you, you can't have your Bible at work. Keep up the good work, keep doing what you're doing."

After our meeting and the break was over, I went back to my desk. I put on my headset and pushed the start button to tell the computer to start auto dialing. I started reciting my script and making sales. I held my Bible in my hand, and I stood up and I turned around and faced the back of the room so while I was reading my Bible, reciting my script and making my sales, I could glance up look into the eyes of my oppressor. I made more sales that day than I'd ever made before.

"if somehow I might move to jealousy my fellow countrymen and save some of them." Romans 11:14 NAS

There's a scripture that says we will make them jealous. "if somehow I might move to jealousy my fellow countrymen and save some of them." Romans 11:14 NAS. There's a reason for that. The idea is that the unsaved will desire to become saved because of the fruit on our tree. This young atheist in the back of the room did not desire to become saved but he did desire to have the sales that I had. I was never able to have a friendly conversation with him because he was such a hater.

I like to think that young atheist would have been influenced in a good way from that experience. I never said anything bad to him or about him. He was always rude to me. I hope that he would be inspired by the way God actually protected me from his complaints. I hope that his seeing me blessed, would inspire him to ask God if he is really real, to come into his life and change him. I do not know what happened to him. I do pray for him when I remember to.

I like to think if he gets to a low point in his life, he would remember his experience battling me at the workplace and recognize that God is alive and well and his power does work and I would hope that the testimony, that witness to him, would be the operative factor that would lead him to reach out and ask God into his life and if he did, that experience I had of God blessing me would be the key that save this one atheist and helped him to become a saved soul.

I fell at the office and re-injured my back and that closed this chapter in my life. My wife continued to work, and I was laid up at home.

My health had deteriorated so much that my Love (my wife Stacy) would put me in the therapy hot tub in the morning, go to work, check on me at lunch to be sure I was still alive, come home at the end of the day and start all over again. It was a sort of living nightmare except that we had each other. I must say if you want to see if someone really loves you try losing everything and not being able to work and see if they stick around. My wife passed the test.

At night I would wake up because of muscle spasms in my back that would wrap around to my torso and make it near impossible to breath. Sometimes my wife was not sure if I was going to survive the night. When I could not breath she would run to the freezer and grab ice that she would pack

118

around my chest and back with towels to catch the dripping water. Then she would run a hot bath. By the time my torso had become numb it would be time to get me into the bath. Sometimes this would happen a couple of times a night. I took so much pain medication it was hard to think. A friend of mine, Beverly Ford, described my complexion as gray.

Nihon Kenko Zoshin Kenkukai (Nikken) had just expanded to the United States a few years before I heard about it. My friend Beverly told me about Nikken, and I was ready to buy because it had worked so well for her. I borrowed $1,700 to purchase a set of everything including the sleep system, a seat cushion, and relax pads for my back and shoes. Within a week the muscle spasms stopped. This allowed me to sleep and it is amazing what a good night's sleep can do for you.

Pretty soon I was talking to everyone about how "we can with Nikken." The easy sales technique was "You try, you like you buy." The first two months we earned enough to pay back the $1,700 I borrowed. Pretty soon we did over $60k in sales in one month and were awarded Platinum level and the 60k club.

Public Speaking started in High school with my sister Alice dragging me to Junior Achievement (JA). I say drag but that was only the first meeting, I loved it, thanks sis. We both earned scholarships to the Dale Carnegie course that prepared me for the next few decades.

People started asking me to speak all over the place. Pretty soon I was doing six cities in six days. The bills were paid, and we started a mail order business with some new Horse Health technology. I was the Basic Horse Wellness expert traveling around to do horse clinics teaching two or three hundred people at a time how to do effective horse massage and electro-acupuncture. While I was at a conference on the

Get STARTED-don't quit!

East coast my wife and I talked on the phone about the horse ranches we had been looking at since the money situation had turned around. She had found one in Monroe, Washington where we were already going to Joe and Linda Knights church that is now pastored by Jeff Knight.

I made a call to the real estate agent and set up a horse ranch shopping trip for the day after I returned to Seattle. The ranch was like a dream come true; it was one of those waking dream moments because God had shown me a vision of this very ranch.

I needed $150,000 for the down payment and I only had $8000 cash on hand. When I met the owner, I told him I did not have the money, but I would get it. We agreed on a price that was a couple hundred thousand less than he was asking and shook hands. We did paper work within a week. Later he told me he just knew I would come up with the money. Six months later we signed papers and moved in.

When we moved in, we only had a dozen horses boarded. Within two months we were full to capacity with over seventy-five horses being boarded. The racetrack was pretty popular for all the boarders. We added a second indoor arena, an outdoor arena and a dressage field as well.

My best friend and his family came to live with us on the ranch. At first in our house and then they got their own mobile home moved to the ranch. We remodeled it together into a beautiful home. It was perfect. God was blessing us with all of our needs being met. My best friend lived with us, so I did not even have to drive anywhere to go see him. We made plans for 007 type "secret squirl" adventures to explore old abandoned mines and take over the world.

My four-tractor garage was a fun workshop to start building up some inventions too. I had an old Scott Air pack that was used by firefighter and Steve told me it was supposed to be good for breathing under water up to ten or fifteen feet. I had been SCUBA diving before, so I said, "Let's find out." We had a dock put in so we could exercise the horses by swimming them in the water. I put on the Scott Air pack and walked out into the water. It worked. I was surprised.

As we were in transition to change the name to Promised Land Estates things changed. My son Isaac was born in January and we thought things would continue to grow. I had made the mistake of investing money that I should have kept in reserve.

It looked like there was no end in sight and then the Y2K challenge came along. There was no real end of the world situation however there was a stock market correction that took place in the spring of 2000.

After the market correction there we many of our clients who had their own barns at home, and they were boarding with us because of the convenience. One client told me she was worth $17 million before the correction and after her portfolio was only worth $7 million so she had to take care of her own horse at home.

My wife was rear ended by a drunk driver, I re-injured my ankle and our two key employees had family emergencies out of town. I turned the riding mower into a wheelchair so I could do the chores every day. Stacy and I started the day by hauling the hay and water to over sixty horses every morning. Then we let them out to pasture, cleaned the stalls, redid the water and brought them dinner. Then rounds again to get the horses and bring them in to the six barns. Finally, we got to bed after midnight and started over again at five am.

After two weeks of this we realized it was not going to get better. My wife and I prayed in the living room of the hundred-year-old farm house that had come with the place. We asked God to help us sell the ranch. I was thankful for the experience of riding horses with my daughter every night before bed. This was an amazing thing to see God move so we could buy the ranch in the first place. Now that we both were injured this had to change, we needed God to help us sell it.

That was in the morning about nine am. Now God always answers prayers, he usually does not work this quickly but here is what happened. At about one pm in the afternoon I had stopped into my office to check phone messages. A knock came at the door. A businessman came in and asked, "You guys ever think about sellin this place?"

Inside I was elated, jumping up and down doing back flips, and yet. Very calmly I said, "What did you have in mind?" A week later we signed papers and walked away from that ranch. Usually it takes two years on the market to sell something like that. What a blessing to see God move that quickly.

Chapter 28

They Shall Walk

"But they that wait on the LORD shall renew their strength; they shall mount up with wings as eagles; they shall run, and not be weary; and They Shall Walk, and not faint."
Isaiah 40:31 KJV

In 2001 a friend of mine, Randy Kaiser, graciously offered me free office space for They Shall Walk, when I told him about my vision to take this out of my garage and get it into the hands of people who needed it. I started networking at the business events and kept running into the problem of my lack of credentials.

I re-enrolled in college at the North Seattle Community College. Scholarships were only easy because I applied for all of them, anything I remotely qualified for.

Within a few days of being on campus talking about what I wanted to do with the LIFESUIT I was presented a key to what used to be the Techtrons Lab for electronics students. I started the Robotics club and opened the first robotics research lab at the community college.

I reached out to the Seattle Robotics Society and got a response from Doug and Charlie. Doug Bell has been a God send with experience as an Electrical Engineer and a programmer. Charlie was an electronics student at the NSCC who also joined the club. Within a few weeks we had a bustling group of students with a variety of interests.

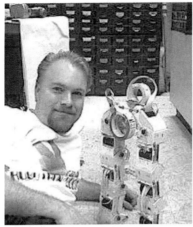

Figure 24 Monty with the LIFESUIT prototype LS6

I built a few prototypes of the LIFESUIT with advice from professors and other members. Pretty soon we had a dedicated crew who were working on the LIFESUIT as well as their projects. Every quarter we had new people join and some stuck around. I had built the first twelve prototypes before taking my first engineering class.

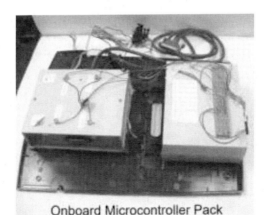

Onboard Microcontroller Pack

Figure 25 Microcontroller mounting system for the LIFESUIT

A couple of weeks after arriving on campus at NSCC I met my favorite English professor Tracy Heinlein. She recruited me to become the managing editor of the Licton Springs Review www.LictonSpringsReview.com literary magazine. With professor Heinlein's guidance, two very committed volunteers (Ara and Alec) and a lot of hard work we won the State competition for Literary magazines. The next year we won the National award under the leadership of the new managing editor Danielle Burhop.

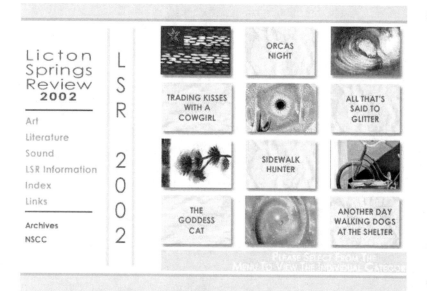

Figure 26 Cover of the Licton Springs Review magazine.

Because of the online e-zine we were accepting new media, David Moody was the tech guy that helped me to handle those submission. When I started the golf club on campus, he became the faculty adviser. As we spent time together, he became one of the biggest fans of They Shall Walk. He also became a sponsor helping fund all the computer and web related expenses.

125

David's contributions to the gift of walking has been priceless. In addition to being a sponsor, David has been a great sounding board for talks about "gum stick PC" control systems for the LIFESUIT and the pros and cons of a Linux operating system vs a micro controller for the LIFESUIT.

We had started to hold an annual: They Shall Walk & Roll-a-thon in Shoreline, Washington (North Seattle on the County line). People would come to walk and with their wheelchairs, bikes and skates to roll to raise money for the LIFESUIT and the exercise partner program at They Shall Walk. Pretty soon anything that walked or rolled started to come. Team Lightning, a skate racing team joined us to roll up and down the Interurban trail that runs parallel to Highway 99. Bicycles, skate boards, scooters, unicycles, strollers, wheelchairs, runners, walkers and rollers made for a great event.

Figure 27 They Shall Walk Volunteers at an Event

Figure 28 the LIFESUIT prototype LS14 being demonstrated by Monty K Reed in Shoreline Washington at an event

127

Figure 29 the LIFESUIT LS14 demonstrated by Monty K Reed going down a curb

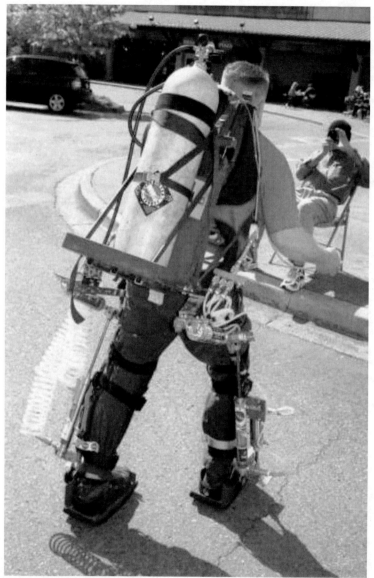

Figure 30 the LIFSUIT LS14 from behind. You can see the SCUBA tank provided by Underwater Sports that powers the whole system. This is a green tech device with a low carbon footprint.

129

The city of Shoreline waived all the fees for the event and even helped promote it as a community event. The Shoreline Chamber of Commerce had already embraced me because of my work as president of the Jaycees and many of the members started exhibiting at our events.

A special "Thank You" goes out to the local businesses for supporting our: They Shall Walk & Roll a thon / Cruise the Ave event.

Les Neu was a Seattle businessman who was intrigued by the LIFESUIT and my story. Les had remembered reading Heinlein's book and was fascinated by what we had done with the Heinlein idea. He was so intrigued he decided to retire and go to work helping to promote They Shall Walk from 2005-2015.

Anything that rolls included cars and a car show component was added. It had become such a popular portion of the They Shall Walk & Roll a thon that it has its own name and website. "Cruise The Ave So, They Shall Walk. Ford has been one of the greatest sponsors for that event.

David started Events Logistics of Washington to help manage the fund-raising and events for They Shall Walk so I could re-focus on directing the research. What a blessing that has been. Before this I was doing fund-raising and research. More than half of my time was spent on finding money. This help made it easier to focus on the research.

A donor offered to pay the rent if we would move the lab to Georgetown. This meant that we went from a 2000 square foot lab in Shoreline to a ten thousand square foot facility just south of downtown Seattle that was made up of two spaces: one was 3000 square feet and the other was 7000 square feet. This added an hour commute to my work schedule and that was a problem on my sick days. We had great staff members come on board and They Shall Walk was able to continue the mission even when I could not get into the lab. Some of the volunteers came to my house for my input when I could not get out of bed.

College and high school students came in to do research under supervision of the volunteer engineers. Most of them were doing senior projects or independent study projects for college credit.

One of my favorite experiences mentoring engineering students was with a student named Andy. He got his first 4.0 grade on his CAD stress analysis project where he predicted the weakest point on the LIFESUIT ankle joint. This spot is exactly where three bolts sheared and caused a failure later.

Every year I would meet with a couple of different senior college engineering classes and the professor would let me pitch to the class some of the projects we had that they could complete in a quarter or a yearlong project. We had over 100 college interns who had worked at the They Shall Walk lab over the years.

I also had lab space that the University of Washington in the Mechanical Engineering Annex near where the race car club had their shop. It was a joy and a pleasure to work with the University of Washington professors, students and staff.

Figure 31 Mr S, Big John, and Monty at the UW Mechanical Engineering Annex were the LIFESUIT LS14 took it's first steps

Chapter 29

The General

I earned my Associates Degree at NorthSeattle.edu aka North Seattle Community College and transferred to the University of Washington on a pre-science degree. My first quarter at the UW I was honored as a Mary Gates Scholar, one of only four thousand in the world. The Undergraduate Research Program (URP) office embraced me and helped me get oriented on campus. I presented at the URP symposium a couple of times in 2006 & 2007. It was a great honor to be featured on the poster for the conference in 2007. I was honored as a NASA Space Grant Scholar as well. I was invited to speak at conferences around the US as well doing oral and poster sessions. One of the greatest honors was being invited to teach a lecture to 500 level class of engineering grad students in Mechatronics at the UW.

One of the first conferences off campus was at the University of Michigan Ann Arbor. "Invest in Access" was the name of the annual conference. When I first was invited to speak, I thought "Great, but I do not have the money to get there." Normal doubt for most full-time undergraduate students.

 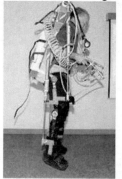 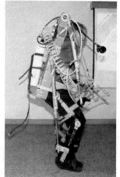

The LIFESUIT prototype LS13 demonstrated jumping up 9 inches.

133

My God is bigger than that and I prayed with my friend Ted Walker who I had met in 2001 when I started going to Philadelphia Church in Seattle. Ted was a regular part of the They Shall Walk team since he was called out by God himself. Ted tells the story better than I can but here goes.

Ted was at church on a Sunday morning, Ted usually has his powered wheelchair all the way up front, so he does not block anyone's access to the alter. The pastor was making a serious point. When Ted felt God was telling him to "Work with Monty." At the thought of going into a robotics lab Ted thought to himself if he were to touch anything electronic it may explode and he started to laugh, out loud.

Figure 32 Monty K Reed and Ted Walker

At that, the Pastor looked down at him wondering why he was laughing at his serious point. As soon as the service was over Ted came to find me. When he told me, he was going to work with me, I looked at him and we both laughed. I asked, "What will you do?" He was not sure, but he knew he was going to work with me, and They Shall Walk. Since then Ted found a great love for the computer and did our emails for several years.

Figure 33Ciara Reed checking the fuel gauge on the LIFESUIT while Monty K Reed walks with Ted Walker rolling

After praying with Ted about the funding for the trip I received an email "Of course we will pay for your travel expenses." I was elated and right after that I had another email "How much is your required honorarium?" Consulting with several professors who all suggested as an undergraduate I should ask for $250, that is what I was going to ask. When I prayed about it, I felt God had a better idea, that I should ask for $750. They gladly paid it.

I went online to try to book the flight to Ann Arbor Michigan and the website rejected my debit card even though I had money in my account. I tried another website and the website locked up. The third website I tried would not accept my card. After calling the bank to be sure I really did have enough money I decided to just go to bed and try again the next day.

That night I had a vision. In the vision I looked around and found myself in a trade show, but it was unlike any I had been to before. Tanks, jets, machine guns, and grenades were all for sale. Soldiers everywhere and sales reps selling war supplies. I could hear sounds off in the distance and smell trade show food. I reached out and touched the side of a nearby armored tank. It was solid, cold and very real.

Then I woke up. I had to know if these kind of trade shows existed so I went online to see what would come up on Bing and google. Sure, enough there were. Of course, there were, how else would the Generals know where to buy the latest new weapons systems. As I searched the listings, I was amazed to see there was a DOD (Department Of Defense) conference just over thirty miles away from the conference in Ann Arbor I was speaking at. The kicker was that the Ann Arbor conference was over on Wednesday morning and the DOD conference started on Wednesday night. This is what they call a sign. After praying some more about this, I felt I should go to this conference to see if I can offer the LIFESUIT to the Army for soldiers who were paralyzed.

After several phone calls and emails, I managed to get a woman on the phone who handles registration for that show. I did not have a current security clearance; I did not have an invitation and she would not give me one. I did not have the $600 it would have cost to register anyway. So, I figured that got me off of the hook for going.

God convicted me otherwise. Because of that, I stepped out in faith and purchased a ticket to get me to Ann Arbor to present Monday and Tuesday and fly back to Seattle on Friday, after the DOD conference was over.

For the next couple of weeks, I tried with no success to get an invitation to that conference. It was too late to change the travel arrangements without paying a penalty, so I headed to the airport with the LIFESUIT in tow.

After arriving in my room, I unpacked the LIFESUIT and reassembled it, did a function test and got my power point ready for the demonstration the next day.

The demonstrations went very well, and I was treated like royalty. I presented a couple of times to students, and professors and did one "In Service" training at the hospital for the doctors, nurses and therapists. I was also honored with a visit to the BCI (Brain Computer Interface) lab on campus. Two of the researchers had been collecting motor function brain activity data for over a decade. I believe that the future controller for the LIFESUIT will be a BCI device the reads thoughts and I believe the data collected in Ann Arbor is the key to unlock the technology.

Wednesday morning, I disassembled the LIFESUIT and packed it back in its shipping crate and headed to the front of the Michigan League hotel to catch the taxi that had been called for me. My wife was able to find a hotel that was "Across the parking lot" from the hotel where the DOD conference was being held. It was not $200 a night like the one the conference was being held in.

When I got into the room, I was exhausted and began to doubt why I was still here. I did not have an invitation, did not have a security clearance and did not have the money to pay for the registration.

I took out my bible and started to read while I was looking for inspiration. I believe the Bible is the inspired word of God and that God will use it to speak to me if I pray, read, meditate on the word, seek God's face and wait upon the Lord.

Laying down for a nap took me into another vision. In the vision I was walking into the lobby of the Hyatt and I looked around. I could see sales people in suits and soldiers in dress uniforms walking around, some sitting and talking. They were everywhere. I saw the entrance to the conference where guards were checking badges off to my right. Off to my left was a table were two men were sitting. They were supposed to introduce me to "The General."

When I woke, I realized it may be my vain imagination or it could have really been a vision from God. When Joseph was invited to have an audience with Pharaoh, he took time to clean up, shave and change his clothes before he did. "Good enough for him, good enough for me." I thought to myself and drew a bath.

Approaching 4PM I put on some business casual clothing and headed over to the Hyatt Regency Hotel. My hotel was in fact "across the parking lot" from the Hyatt, the problem was that it was over a half mile shopping mall parking lot. I trekked across the parking lot, enjoying the fresh air and the exercise across this vast parking lot. There was a lot to see; lots of cars and a few people going to and from the stores in the mall.

As I walked into the Hyatt lobby, I noticed things were a little different than in the vision, but most things were similar enough. In the vision the conference was on the left in the East wing of the hotel, and in reality, it was to the right in the West wing. I walked towards the entrance to the DOD conference.

As I stood there, I looked over at the guards who were checking badges at the door. One person was showing his passport even though he had a conference registration name badge. I realized there was no way I was going to be slipping past those guards to crash this party. A feeling of calm overtook me when I realized a lot of the background noises I could hear were in the vision. Even the sports bar behind me with a football game playing.

I tried to stand about where I was in the vision. The guards were on my right, a table with one guy sitting at it was directly in front of me and off to my left was a table and four chairs with three guys sitting at it. In my vision there were two men not three.

"When thou art departed from me to day, then thou shalt find two men ..." 1 Samuel 10:2 KJV

I figured three was close and this was the table. I walked over and introduced myself to the three guys and sat down. The man on my left was talking to the other two guys about armor piercing ammunition and body armor while he gestured with his hands. He stopped mid-sentence with his gesturing hand suspended in the air and turned to look at me. His gaze looked down from my face to my chest, scanning to see that I did not have a DOD conference name badge like he and his friends did. "Excuse me, who did you say you were again?" I explained that I had developed an exoskeleton that will help paralyzed soldiers to walk. He turned to the other two guys and said, "I am sorry, I have got to go." He got up and left without even a glance at me.

Now there we two men sitting at this table with me just like in the vision.

The other two men turned back to me and leaned in as they asked me to tell them more. I shared my story of developing the robotic suit and that I had just presented at a conference in Ann Arbor. I told them that I was hoping to talk to someone at the conference about the LIFESUIT robotic suit for paralyzed soldiers.

"Do you have it here with you?" Hans asked, "the robotic suit, do you have it here?" I told him I was staying across the parking lot at the other hotel and I had it there, in my room. "Would you bring it here tomorrow?" they both asked. "Will you put it on and demonstrate it here at the hotel?" Hans asked a little more excited. I assured them that I could and calmly asked "What did you have in mind?"

"Well, if you will put it on and bring it here tomorrow..." Hans leaned over and whispered to his friend something and they both leaned forward and said in stereo "We will introduce you to the General."

The hair on my neck stood on end, the tingling ran up and down my spine. I did not even need to know who this General was, he was important enough for God to show me in a vision and these guys were going to get me the audience I needed with him.

Hans told me to be back over at the hotel at 4:50pm exactly because that is when the session gets out "Meet me in the front of the hotel on the West end." He gave me his cell phone and told me to call him when I got there.

140

Get STARTED-don't quit!

I went back to my room, unpacked the LIFESUIT and reassembled it. I was all out of cash and had no money left in my bank account. I ordered a pizza because I knew it would keep at room temperature and I could live on it until Friday and they took credit cards.

The next day I spent working on my research in my room and I took time to pray until it was time to go meet the General.

I fired up the LIFESUIT, climbed into it and walked to the elevator. When I walked through the lobby of my hotel, I got a lot of looks from people wondering what it was.

I would have liked to have taken a taxi or even a bus, but I had no cash left. A hundred feet from my hotel with over a half mile to go, I realized I did not have enough fuel to make it all the way to the Hyatt, and to demonstrate it to the General. I had to choose to use the fuel for the demonstration, not getting to the demonstration. I was going to have to put the system into "Neutral Gear" and walk under my own power. That meant I would have to carry the LIFESUIT myself with every step.

Just then a police car pulled up. "Hey who are you and what is that thing?" the officer in the passenger seat asked. After I told him what it was, I mentioned that I was trying to get to the Hyatt as I pointed to it. I was hoping maybe they would help me in some way. He responded, "this is not a very safe neighborhood and you will probably get mugged." With that they drove off.

I started to doubt if I was supposed to be here and if I was really supposed to meet the General. It started to rain. Now I was cold, tired, and I felt beaten as I struggled to walk wearing the eighty-six-pound LIFESUIT.

141

"And he saith unto them, Why are ye fearful, O ye of little faith? Then he arose, and rebuked the winds and the sea; and there was a great calm."
Mathew 8:26

I realized I was supposed to be here, and I was supposed to meet the General. I saw it in a vision, those men were real, and Hans was expecting me. It was clear and obvious that Satan himself was pulling out the big guns to try to stop me. The Devil must have a reason he does not want me there. I started to pray.

"Oh, heavenly Father you are mighty and great. You deserve all praise and glory and honor. You are awesome. Lord God you told me to ask and I shall receive, and I am asking now for your help in getting me to the Hyatt to meet the General. I believe your visions are real and that your word is true. Lord God almighty I ask you to bring me a truck to get me to that hotel. In the name of Jesus Christ of Nazareth, I ask you Lord God to bless me." I continued to pray as if it were all up to God and I continued to walk in the rain towards that hotel as if it were all up to me. I was expecting God would deliver.

Within five minutes of praying that prayer a red Ford F150 extended cab pickup truck approached me from the South. It stopped about twenty feet away from me and a young man called out from the passenger window to ask what I was doing and what was I wearing. I told him.

Then with boldness I spoke, realizing that I had asked God for a truck and here was a truck. "Hey, can you help me out?" I asked. "What do you need?" he asked. I laid it out. "Pick me up, put me in your truck and take me to that hotel over there." as I pointed to the Hyatt that was still a half mile away.

Four young men got out of the truck, they looked nineteen, muscle bound wearing t-shirts and jeans all with crew cuts. They could have been Marines, Rangers, football players or angels. Today they were my angels and an answer to prayer. With no effort the guys lifted me and the LIFESUIT into the back of the pickup. I hung on as they drove me to the hotel in the rain.

As they unloaded me, I noticed limo's and people in tuxedos and gowns going into the hotel. The LIFESUIT at the time was still very loud when I powered it up and started to walk. I looked at my watch and realized it was 4:46pm. If God had not sent that truck, there is no way I would have made this meeting with Hans. I called him and he walked out at 4:52pm, grabbed my arm and we walked into the hotel.

He brought me back to the table we had met at twenty-four hours before. "Wait here, I will be right back with the General." In a couple of minutes Hans was introducing me the General who was in charge of Army research. He told me "You got four minutes."

Twenty minutes later, we were still talking about how the LIFESUIT could help paralyzed soldiers to walk. Wounded warriors could wear a LIFESUIT and stay active duty, they would not be required to become disabled Veterans. Most would learn to walk again.

The General wanted to know if the LIFESUIT could help soldiers on the battlefield to carry all of the technology that had been developed for them? One of the repeated themes for this conference specifically was how to deal with the weight of all of the equipment that is being developed for soldiers. The current load for one man could be five hundred pounds because there is so much gear. I explained that the LIFESUIT is designed for paralyzed people to walk but it was based on a battlefield powered armor.

I had designed a Rescue Worker Model of the LIFESUIT that would allow firefighters to dig survivors out of the rubble of a collapsed building. That system is designed to lift over a thousand pounds, so a five-hundred-pound load is not a problem.

"General Smith will contact you about a proposal, we are going to do some work together." He assured me and went on to his next meeting.

Hans came over to me and asked, "Are you up for a little adventure?" He explained that the guards may not like it but he had to get me inside the conference, there was over fifteen people he wanted me to meet. Majors, Generals and people who handled procurement for the military. "We are going to go into the conference, act like you are supposed to be there, when the guards chase us just keep walking and go right in and meet with that guy in the blue uniform" as Hans pointed him out he asked "do you see him?" I agreed to do as he said, and we started walking towards the conference doors.

"And he said unto them, Behold, when ye are entered into the city, there shall a man meet you... follow him into the house where he entereth in"
Luke 22:10 KJV

The guards did yell out and two of them did start to chase towards us. Hans yelled out to them "It's okay, he is with me." and held up his conference name badge. The guards objected and demanded that I needed to have a badge too. "He is part of the conference; this equipment needs to be seen by...." We had already gone inside forty feet and Hans pushed me gently towards the inside of the conference. He turned and confronted the guards. Inside I was greeted by a Soldier who introduced me to two dozen people. Hans joined me and I spent a couple of hours meeting people and talking to them about the LIFESUIT robotic exoskeleton.

Today you will read about robotic exoskeletons being developed by the Army to allow soldiers to carry loads on the battlefield and to lift 200-pound payloads onto aircraft. With functional exoskeletons soldiers will be able to carry a full load of gear and the batteries to go with them. I look forward to the day that Wounded Warriors will be able to use the LIFESUIT to return to work and to get the gift of walking.

Chapter 30

The Lab

My lab space at the UW Mechanical engineering building and the lab space at NSCC had been over grown with LIFESUIT prototypes. At this point we had thirteen of them and were working on the next three. We located our new lab in Shoreline and moved prototypes from eight storage units, my basement & garage, NSCC lab and the Lab at the University of Washington. Now all of the work was in one place.

Within a couple of years, we had outgrown that two thousand square foot lab and needed to relocate. Several volunteers, donors and sponsors over the years had told me I should look at Georgetown. "Located 5 miles south of downtown Seattle, Georgetown is Seattle's oldest residential neighborhood."

After two months of prayer with a few two- and three-day fasts tossed in I had a revelation on a Sunday after church. I sat down for lunch and within an hour I was; 1. invited to speak at the Georgetown Neighborhood Association, 2. preach to the Georgetown Community Church, and 3.I was invited to look at a three thousand square foot commercial space in Georgetown. By the end of that week I had spoken at the Community Church and the Neighborhood Association and taken a look inside the new commercial space. A couple of days after that, God provided the funding for the new rent at the lab.

Just a few years after that we have outgrown that space as well. We moved into the new space as I publish the first edition of this book. They Shall Walk Institute was being positioned to handle more interns, more students, more patients and more volunteers than ever before.

146

The NASA Space grant program put me in contact with
hundreds of amazing minds.

*Astronaut Janet Kavandi, UW alumna and chief of the astronaut office in Houston, with
WSGC Director Robert Winglee and Space Grant student researchers.*

Washington marks NASA 's 50th anniversary

The Mary Gates Community of Scholars was another
amazing networking opportunity.

As we grew, I went to tour the CMC (Christian Medical
College) in Vellore India, located one hundred miles inland
form Chennai India. This trip could have it's own book all
together so I will share these stories in another volume.

My friend Derek Forseth introduced me to Tim Swager who
had a roommate in college who was a top spinal surgeon at
the CMC and was my host and guide for this trip.

Figure 34 CMC Vellore India Hospital LIFESUIT Team with Monty K Reed

I met amazing people. The staff there were treating over six thousand outpatients a day. Today they treat over eight thousand outpatients and two thousand inpatients daily.

Figure 35 Monty K Reed at the CMC in Vellore India at the Rehab Medicine department

I toured the CMC to give lectures on the LIFESUIT and the LIFESUIT therapy. I worked with the doctors and medical students there. I was also honored to speak at the Voorhees College to the entire student body.

Using CAD we developed new versions of the LIFESUIT without building them. The FDA approval was lagging behind by over a decade. The LIFESUIT we developed could jump nine inches off of the ground as well as ascend and descend stairs. The government authorities require that medical versions of the LIFESUIT have these advanced functions turned off. If you want to ascend or descend stairs or jump with a LIFESUIT you have to do it outside of the USA.

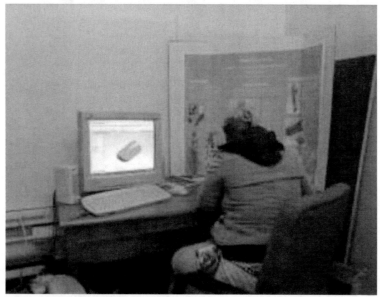

Figure 36 CAD station in the lab where we work out designs for the LIFESUIT

For this reason, we are now working on a NON-Medical version of the LIFESUIT called the FUNSUIT.

149

Figure 37 They Shall Walk Volunteer Crew at the finish line of the Saint Patrick's Day Dash fun run

I decided to go after a Guinness Book World Record for the land speed distance record for exoskeletons. In order to qualify I had to prove we were not a one of a kind and prove that I achieved a world record. So, I gathered information on the other labs that were developing other exoskeletons based on our designs and publications. I registered for the Saint Patrick's Day Dash fun run with the competitive timing chip option with my registration. I let the Guinness Book people know that there were going to be ten thousand witnesses and we would have an official time recorded by the third-party timing chip company. I also made sure to hand write and deliver press releases to the TV and Radio stations in town.

150

The world record was awarded and published in the 2018 edition of the Guinness Book of World Records page 75.
Land Distance Record 3.4 miles in 90 minutes.
Land Speed Record 2.5 mph.
High Jump of twelve inches.

Figure 38 Saint Patrick's Day Dash Fun Run finish line. Ciara, Monty, Isaac & Chance

151

Chapter 31

Going Back

My wife and two kids went on a trip to the Robogames in the Bay area to demonstrate the LIFESUIT robotic exoskeleton. From there we drove south to USC so I could interview for a Graduate position in a robotics program.

Figure 39 Monty, Jamie from Mythbusters, Stacy and Ciara. photo taken at the Robogames

We went to the hospital where I was trapped for a year at what used to be Fort Ord. The Army base was closed now, and abandoned buildings were everywhere. We drove around to see all of the places I could remember and told the family some stories.

Then I found the hospital, we pulled up in front and I did a little dance on the grass. It's funny, because it's no longer a hospital, it is a Department of Defense Language Institute.

152

There was one of those Marines who is supposed to stare straight ahead and not be distracted. He couldn't help but to laugh at me dancing around on the grass. I felt like the music was in me. I worshipped God on that lawn that day. I raised my arms high into the sky and praised the living God that he had healed me and set me free from that prison of paralysis. I thanked him for honoring me with the assignment of being the founder and research director of They Shall Walk www.TheyShallWalk.org I thanked him for providing the people and the resources he had to build the first fourteen prototypes of the LIFESUIT and I thanked him for the burden of giving the gift of walking with the LIFESUIT therapy.

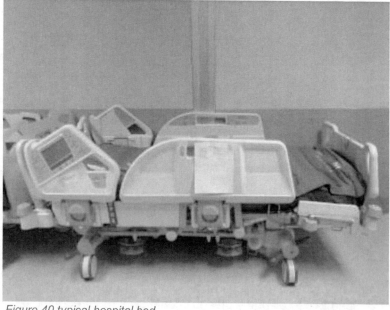

Figure 40 typical hospital bed

Chapter 32

Saving Lives: Changing Lives

153

Get STARTED-don't quit!

When I was in Saint Louis presenting my work at a conference, one of the nurse's had a comment during the question and answer session. She made the point that my work has already given hope to patients who have lost their ability to walk. Patients had told her that they are looking forward to getting a LIFESUIT robotic exoskeleton so they can get around when their legs are failing them.

I have been frustrated sometimes when my work is not proceeding as fast as I would like or when the work is going well and there is not enough money to pay for the next step.

Whenever I get discourage or frustrated, I remind myself that this project is bigger than just me there are committed volunteers around the globe working to help me give the gift of walking. It used to be just me and God but now it is a team effort. All I have to do is go to my email inbox and there will be something motivating that comes in.

A teenage boy from Singapore emailed me to share his story. He was paralyzed as long as he could remember. Recently he had become depressed because he could not go to the mall with his friends and he could not play soccer. He had decided to kill himself and was trying to figure out how to take his own life when he found a news clip about the LIFESUIT. After going to the website, he realized this was real and that he would walk someday. He told me this had given him hope and that he could wait for this. The LIFESUIT robotic exoskeleton gave him a reason to live.

A twenty-two-year-old man emailed me to thank me for doing this work. His twenty-one-year-old wife had been paralyzed in a car accident a year before and every night he had been scouring the internet for something, anything that would give her hope. When he found my website, he was elated. Sharing the website www.TheyShallWalk.org with his wife

154

made her smile and lifted both of their spirits. They were excited that someday soon they would have a LIFESUIT she could use to excise and eventually learn to walk again.

A woman in New Jersey wrote to me because her pre-teen daughter used to ice skate before the accident, and she wanted to know more about the FUNSUIT version of the LIFESUIT. This version of the LIFESUIT can be used by able bodied persons to learn muscle memory for exercise. It is also a sport model of the LIFESUIT that paralyzed people will be able to use to do fun sports like ice skating, golf, tennis etc...

Figure 41 Dr. Steve Stiens and Monty K Reed

When I was at the Robogames event a couple of years ago we had just reassembled the LIFESUIT after shipping it down and began testing it to lift weights.

This version of the LIFESUIT has manipulators (robot term for hands or arms) that could lift a barbell with a couple of hundred pounds on it. I was test lifting small loads and then, for fun I picked up a barrel and tossed it across the open floor of the room. As I turned around, I caught the face of a twelve-year-old girl in a wheelchair watching me with glee. She could see that the LIFESUIT will not only allow her to walk but she would be able do fun stuff too.

After a demonstration at the State Fair I received an email from a father of a teenager who was paralyzed. He told me that after seeing the LIFESUIT demonstration his son's attitude about life had changed. It used to be hard to get him motivated to do homework or even care for himself. After realizing he has a chance to walk again when he gets a LIFESUIT his attitude about school, household chores, and life had become brighter.

Sitting at one of my favorite coffee shop / bookstore commons area in Lake Forest Park I was introduced to a ND (Naturopathic Doctor). A couple of minutes after she left, she returned with another woman in tow. The ND introduced her to me, as I handed her one of the They Shall Walk brochures she asked, "Does this have anything to do with the museum in Georgetown?" I assured her it did, and she answered back "Are you Monty Reed, the guy who started this?" I smiled "Yes..." she interrupted me "We talked last year you helped me with Emily, she is doing so much better" as she reached to put her arms around me, I hugged her back and invited her to take a lab tour on Monday night or the second Saturday of the month. These tours are no longer available because we have closed the lab and are raising money for a newer better research lab facility.

This used to be a strange happening, but I am getting used to it. This is one of the reasons I would encourage you to Get STARTED - don't quit. The most important is to get started and start asking for help. You will be amazed at how many people will want to help when you ask.

"Your Assignment Is What God Has Created You To Do."

Ask yourself: What angers me? What person or group of people do I have a passion to help? Who is it that I really want to see succeed? All of these questions will help you to determine your gifting and your purpose or "your assignment." I pray God will reveal to you his plans and purposes for your life. I pray God will show you what he made you for. Every person has unique gifts, talents, and experiences that make you who you are.

Sometimes we go through tragedy in our lives, horrible things happen to us. I believe surviving those times and experiences qualify us to help mentor others to come through similar experiences. I think of tragedy like a landmine field that we find ourselves in. We were taught that if you notice the paratroopers below you are blowing up as they hit the ground aim for one of the holes because the bomb has already gone off. When you are in the middle of the mine field look for someone who has made it out already. Ask them to guide you out by showing you the way they made it. This is why I believe mentoring is so important.

Find a mastermind group of people you can trust who want you to succeed and meet with them weekly to be accountable to achieving your goals and dreams.

Your life has made you especially qualified to do something. Ask God to reveal to you what you are to be doing. Sometimes seasons change and your assignment may change as well. You may have been doing something for twenty years and it is a new season. Ask God to help you. Wait on the Lord to reveal his plans and purposes for your

157

life. Seek answers in the written word of God by reading the Bible. Pray to the Lord God almighty, ask in the name of Jesus Christ of Nazareth for an answer. Invite the Holy Spirit of Truth to dwell with you and in you.

Write to me I will pray for you and your assignment in life.

Figure 42 Nazareth in Israel photo by Monty K Reed

Chapter 33

The LIFESUIT Robotic Exoskeleton: the gift of walking

The author (Monty K Reed) envisioned LIFESUIT therapy in 1986 while being hospitalized for a spinal cord injury as a result of a parachute accident while serving with the US Army Airborne Rangers. The research started while he was an inpatient at the hospital and continues today at the world headquarters of, They Shall Walk. The program is based on visions he had in the hospital that shows a four-decade plan and thirty-six prototypes of the LIFESUIT robotic exoskeleton. At this writing we are half way into that plan.

The LIFESUIT Robotic Exoskeleton is a robotic suit that allows paralyzed people to walk and exercise. It has been developed to be placed in hospital physical therapy (PT) clinics where patients will go three times a week or more to exercise and learn to walk again. It will be helpful for anyone with a spinal cord injury (SCI), stroke, multiple sclerosis (MS), cerebral palsy (CP), polio, advanced age and any other conditions that may limit mobility. Many people who have joint replacements will also be able to use the LIFESUIT therapy for rehabilitation and to speed their recovery.

Eventually it will be available at gyms and health clubs as well. Numerous studies have demonstrated that "Exercise Based Therapy" improves the health of paralyzed people and that some will learn to walk again as a direct result. The primary issue with exercise-based therapy is the cost.

Traditional exercise-based therapy for paralyzed patients is performed by suspending a paralyzed person over a treadmill while physical therapists manipulate the patient's legs by lifting each leg forward and setting them on the belt of the treadmill. The movement of the treadmill moves the leg back and the therapist repeats the action. If this is done three or more times a week the patient has a positive benefit. The problem is the cost of three physical therapists for one patient. Typical insurance will not pay for that therapy yet.

Figure 43 Dr. Steven Stiens and Monty K Reed in the lab

This type of therapy was pioneered by Dr. Steven Stiens in Seattle, WA. He named the therapy "Weight-Supported Ambulation." He used a modified parachute harness to support a paraplegic over a treadmill to exercise. A similar therapy was devised by Daniel Ferris in Ann Arbor Michigan. Patients were placed on a treadmill with therapy students lifting the legs forward onto the treadmill. Most of the patients (80%) improved mobility in some way.

The LIFESUIT robotic exoskeleton will allow paralyzed patients to benefit from these therapy models without the high cost of three or more physical therapists per patient or the use of treadmills. Once you have robots doing a job, they work without taking break, they do not complain, do not take time off and do not have a union... yet! Ai is coming, beware.

I envision every rehabilitation, sports medicine, exercise and physical therapy clinic around the world having five to ten LIFESUIT therapy stations to serve hundreds of patients each. A new patient will work with the therapist for the first few sessions to learn how to operate the system and then after that they will be able to operate the LIFESUIT robotic exoskeleton on their own. One therapist can supervise five to ten patients at the same time. The cost savings will be incredible.

I believe the LIFESUIT therapy will allow most paralyzed people to learn to walk again in as little as two years. A patient walking in a LIFESUIT robotic exoskeleton will allow their nervous system to reconnect to the muscles and the brain and remap connections. It has been demonstrated with stroke patients and some incomplete spinal cord injury patients. Imagine the cost savings to the insurance and healthcare system if most mobility impaired people could return to work in as little as two years.

Figure 44 Monty K Reed in the LIFESUIT prototype LS13 Jumping 9 inches off of the ground at Robogames

LIFESUIT prototypes can jump nine inches off of the ground.

www.GetSTARTED-dontquit.com

The LIFESUIT is not limited to being used on a treadmill that takes valuable floor space in PT clinics. In the first couple of weeks a patient could use the treadmill to get comfortable with the controls. After training is complete, the patients can use the LIFESUIT to walk the hallways of the hospital or clinic.

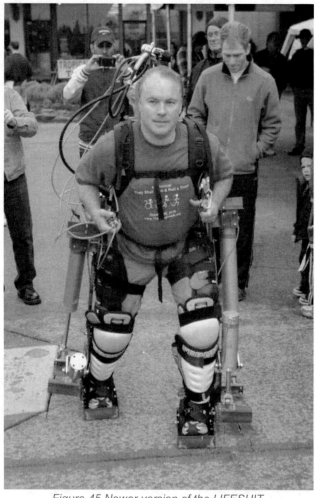

Figure 45 Newer version of the LIFESUIT

163

Because of the "Mimic and Playback" system I pioneered to train the LIFESUIT, therapists and patients can work together one on one for the first two weeks of use. The therapist wears a lightweight sensor suit (aka telemetry suit) that is connected to the powered suit the patient is wearing. In real time the therapist will do the exercises the patient needs to perform as they have a conversation about how it works. The two can talk about how the session is going while they work together. The "Mimic and Playback" system has a "Parallel" mode that allows the therapist to stand alongside the patient. There is a "Mirror" mode that allows the patient and therapist to face each other during the training session.

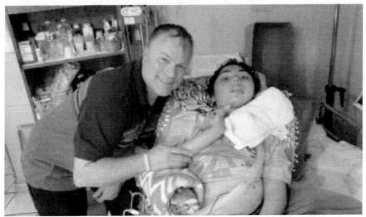

Figure 46 Monty with Benny who has been paralyzed since age 4 is waiting for funds to be raised for his LIFESUIT that he will be able to use to exercise while laying down and then later stand up and walk. His dream is to walk again. You can donate to help him get a LIFESUIT.

After the exercises are recorded for that patient they will be stored in a "Patient Profile" on a clinic's computer network. The patient will have a log in or swipe card that we call the LIFESUIT drivers' license. The therapist has complete override control to prevent any patient from over doing it.

As a clinic or a therapist records these exercise routines they can be stored and shared with They Shall Walk headquarters and other LIFESUIT therapy sites around the world.

The organization includes doctors, nurses, therapists, engineers, technicians and high school and college students. Most of them work independently around the world. Around the country and in other parts of the world where researchers are working to advance the technology of the LIFESUIT robotic exoskeleton. They Shall Walk is a non-profit medical research organization committed to developing technology that will improve the quality of life of paralyzed people. The LIFESUIT is the main project; however, it is not the only one.

They Shall Walk has also been developing other technology such as integrated robotics systems that help around the kitchen, the home and the workplace. Other technology is being developed to help patients transfer from wheelchairs to the LIFESUIT and back and forth to a seat, a commode, shower, desk chair or a bed. Other simple therapy devices are being developed as well that include passive exercise for single joints. Anything you may could imagine or read about in science fiction that could improve a paralyzed persons' life you may hear about at They Shall Walk; all we do is make science fiction real. We take the fiction out of Science Fiction.

The LIFESUIT has a joystick controller allowing anyone who can drive a powered wheelchair to drive a LIFESUIT.

If the FDA approval process cost is similar to the two-wheeled balancing wheelchair it will run over a hundred million dollars before paralyzed people in the United States will be able to use this system here. We are raising that money and you can help by making a donation or volunteering your time as an attorney, paralegal, doctor, therapist or a nurse.

Other countries have already tentatively approved the LIFESUIT therapy and people will be able to travel to places like India to learn to walk again. Inside the United States the LIFESUIT technology is limited to the non-stairclimbing and non-jumping functions.

After the therapy model is installed at one thousand sites around the world, They Shall Walk will focus on delivering the home use model that can be used around the house and the workplace. We call this the FUNSUIT and it is a NON-Medical version of the LIFESUIT.

You can buy a LIFESUIT devices from a dozen companies now. There are over 300 paralyzed people who use powered exoskeletons everyday now instead of wheelchairs. You can join them.

They Shall Walk has developed a hybrid system that incorporates the best of the wheelchair and the LIFESUIT exoskeleton together. A paralyzed person can drive the LIFESUIT wheelchair around and when they come to an obstacle or they want to walk for exercise they simply push a button and the LIFESUIT stands up and the wheels fold up like landing gear. When they are ready to roll, they push another button and the wheels deploy and the system converts back into a wheelchair.

The home use model is the best of both worlds, people will have mobility and passive exercise-based therapy at the same time. All they need to do is exercise and live their lives while they benefit at the same time.

After the LIFESUIT home use model is completed and available the research focus will turn to the development of the Nanotech Biosynthetic Muscle Fiber Suit. This suit will be developed using fibers that are part living tissue and part synthetic material. Every thread in the fabric will expand and contract like muscles. Muscles are more efficient motors than

166

anything we have created so far. The fibers will be so small they cannot be seen with the naked eye.

Judges Choice Maker Booth Award.

The Biosynthetic Muscle Fiber Suit will look very much like a wet suit and can be worn under the clothes. Initially they will be fed with fuel pods that include nourishment and collect waste. The fuel pods will be changed like a battery.

Eventually hybrid versions of the Biosynthetic Muscle Fiber LIFESUIT will incorporate animal and plant tissue that will feed off of each other.

In the future a paralyzed patient will wake up in the morning and call out "Come here boy" and the LIFESUIT will crawl over to them and wrap itself around them. It will read their thoughts and when they think about standing up and walking the LIFESUIT will take them where they want to go. It will be available in all flesh tones and nearly undetectable to the untrained eye. It will be water proof so the wearer can take it into the shower and wear it in the rain. The biosynthetic LIFESUIT will be matched with a wearer for life or until the person learns to walk again.

To get the LIFESUIT and the gift of walking to the world it will only take $200 million. If every American gave one dollar we would have enough. That will allow for the infrastructure, the staff and the logistics to get the job done. This will allow for any hospital or clinic that wants one to have it and any patient who wants to use one to have access to it. When you consider the ADA (Americans with Disabilities Act) the LIFESUIT should be available to any American who wants it. We are working on that and we would love to see the LIFESUIT available to give the gift of walking to anyone who wants it.

Many paralyzed people have been looking for a cure and many believe a cure is coming. When a cure is developed for paralysis, all of those people will need to learn to walk again and the LIFESUIT will be a complimentary therapy to work with other cures as they are developed. For many paralyzed people, the LIFESUIT therapy is the cure.

If you are reading this book and the LIFESUIT is not available in your country yet, please ask your physical therapist or rehabilitation doctor to help you get access to one.

Consider getting involved: Advocate, Volunteer & Donate.

The greatest honor to date has been having a paper published in IEEE in 2014. "LIFESUIT Exoskeleton Gives the Gift of Walking so They Shall Walk"

Chapter 34

Futurist Papers

MANA BOX: In 1976 I envisioned a system of combining plants and living animal tissue to convert animal waste into food via photosynthesis. I called this the "Mana Box" and it would use Nano technology to connect the hoses. The vision part is that the term nanotechnology did not come around until 1990. I did not have the term nanotech; however, I did have the design.

AUTOMATIKITCHEN: in 1978 I envisioned a system that would set the table, clear the table, wash the dishes and put them away. Push a button and the robots set the table for two casual setting. Push another button and then the robots set a formal seven course meal for twelve. They even expand the table size and get out the extra chairs.

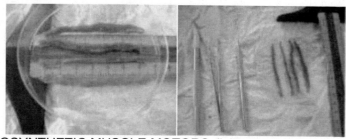

BIOSYNTHETIC MUSCLE MOTORS: living muscle tissue combined with synthetic materials result in living muscles that can perform more work than any manufactured machine. Living muscle is more powerful than other machines. These motors will be powered by "Pods" that include an electric power source as well as food for the muscles and a reservoir for some waste elements that can be recycled outside of the motor's environment. These biosynthetic muscles can be grown in a dish in about eight weeks. The future trick will be to embed nanotech scale microcontrollers. The future version of the LIFESUIT will be made of a fabric that will look like a wetsuit and be worn under the clothes.

169

BIOSYNTHETIC INNER EAR: For those who have lost the ability to balance this synthetic copy of the inner ears semicircular canals can be surgically implanted in an operation similar to the cochlear implant for hearing impaired. When the inner ear is damaged from fever, injury or disease this simple and complex system can be replaced.

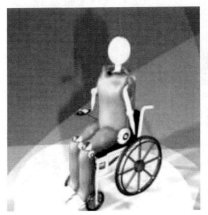 

FUNSUIT EXOSKELETON: For those who have ever wanted to just feel the power of an ironman suit; all you need to do is put this on and start to play. The FUNSUIT can lift over one thousand pounds, dance and even play soccer. It is not designed especially for paralyzed people however if a paralyzed person wants to use it, we would never dream of violating the Americans with Disabilities Act and tell them we are too prejudice to let them.

This FUNSUIT will come with a preemptive lawsuit against any public, private or government entity that may show any discrimination against a paralyzed person who just wants to have fun.

170

SUPER LEARN PODS: This is a new type of meditation chamber that uses a combination of environmental controls, sound, synthetic smells, tastes, lights, videos and variable speed audios to teach subjects at a high speed. The first topic that will be taught to most users will be speed reading. Most people will be able to consume a four-year college degree by using this device part time in one year.

EZ TRANSFER: For paralyzed people who need to transfer from a wheel chair to any other seated position this device will assist them. You will have to wait until the movie comes out. We built a prototype and tested it. It works and could retail for less than two thousand dollars.

SELF GROWING STEAK: Without any genetic Frankenstein type of work you can easily grow beef, lamb or goat without ever killing anything. In fact, you could find the absolute best beef cow and never have to kill it. You could simply get a

171

single cell sample and inject it into a freshly fertilized quail egg and "presto-chango" and eight weeks later you will have a steak roll in the shape of a roast that just needs to have a slice cut off, every so often so it does not get too big. A little electric stim and you can adjust the firmness and tenderness of the meats. No animal ever needs to die again. I developed this technology for the astronauts in my life and realized this could be used to feed the masses in the world.

KASHMIR KLOTHS: Natural clothing that comes from Kashmir. Kashmir is a place. This socially responsible business model is designed to make sure most of the profits go back to the mountains of Kashmir and to the artisans whose families have been creating this fabric for thousands of years. Scarves, shirts, blankets and rugs of pure Kashmir will make a difference for the consumer and the artists who create these clothes and fabrics.

BRAIN FOOD FEAST: Natural powdered foods that are customized for a specific person's health concerns. Using full panel blood work, it is possible to determine the allergy levels for 600 foods. DNA now can determine a variety of pre-dispositions toward certain health problems. Other simple blood and urine tests can determine needed elevations in consumption of certain foods. With these advanced testing being so affordable it should be easy to create a powdered food that supplies most of the nutrition needs for the individual. This could easily be used to make daily smoothies. This liquid food will get to the cells on a lightning fast timetable and have quick effect to the longer life, health and wellness of the consumer. Why not have a super shake or smoothie that tastes good and is good for you. It will be flavored with food. Thomas Edison said something to the effect of "Food will be thy medicine." With a combination of just 200 foods it could easily be done to customize a brain food powder or a muscle food powder etc… depending on the needs of the consumer. Eighty percent of the people alive today want to be healthy.

Get STARTED-don't quit!

WATCH: Wrist Acupuncture Therapy Cold Heat device for curing and preventing carpal tunnel syndrome. Wear this watch device throughout the day and get: massage, electromassage, electro acupuncture, ultrasound, heat and cold therapy.

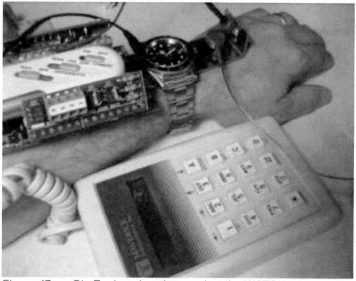

Figure 47 my Bio Engineering class project the WATCH

PREPAID SIM CARDS. Ditch your phone bill by purchasing a five-year sim card and just stop paying all the extra fees. An average family would save over two thousand dollars per phone by purchasing this type of technology.

SLAMCOOKING with FIVE MINUTE MEALS that are actually good for you. This is the new food supply using freeze dried foods that are picked fresh and kept full of vitamins and nutrients, so you no longer need to take vitamins or supplements. With this new food, your food will be your medicine. You can get groceries delivered to your door. Major appliance manufacturers are developing new appliances for use with freeze dried foods.

Figure 48 Monty K Reed at Thrive Headquarters. Thrive provides the best freeze-dried foods for Slam Cooking

Figure 49 Monty K Reed & Chef Todd Leonard Chef of the year 2018-2019 and he has helped develop many of the SlamCooking recipes.

174

Chapter 35

Conclusion

Using what I call "Future Past Tense" I want you to project yourself forward in your mind and Imagine, if all things were possible, how your life would be different? Imagine over the next five years you make all of the right decisions, then you look back over the last half decade and describe your new life, describe your perfect day. Write it out from the moment you wake, a play by play description of how a typical day would go for you.

Here is how mine would go:
Birds chirping and the sound of a river running with other nature sounds slowly getting louder as an artificial sunrise brightens up my bedroom. Opening my eyes brings elation at the new day dawning. Off in the distance I can hear the sound of my robot waiter bringing me a cup of coffee made to perfection, just the way I like it. The smell of coffee and essential oils fills the air. I thank God for this day and for the last few decades of amazing life. I reflect for a moment on all of the things I am thankful for. A projector is putting up on the wall a slide show of many of those things I am thankful for. After that set of slides the next list of affirmations go by reminding me to be forward focused on my assignment given to me by God.

I enjoy my coffee, pray and imagine how amazing the next few hours and the rest of this day will go. Perfectly placed slippers and a robe help me to rise from my bed and go to my "Prayer Closet." This is a special room in my home, it is a bedroom that is designated for God. It is my place to go and to pray. It is not an office or actual bedroom that is also used for prayer, it is a dedicated space that belongs to the Holy Spirit. It is a room that is just used for prayer. Imagine the closet in the movie "War Room" and then move that concept to a full-size bedroom.

175

I enter the prayer closet and the lights automatically brighten a bit. Just enough so I can see to get to the low table where I kneel and pray. There is a bible, a concordance a bible dictionary and two notebooks with a bunch of pens and pencils. The notebooks are the Steno style with graph paper in case God gives me inventions that need to be drawn. The notebook on the right is the "God" notebook. The one on the left is my "Journal" notebook.

Let me tell you why I have two notebooks. Have you ever found when you are trying to pray, I mean really focus on praying and you find all of these distractions coming into your mind? You start thinking about all of those things you need to do as soon as you get done praying. I used to just try to shove those thoughts out of my mind but how well does that work? Not at all, right. So, I have found the best way to deal with those distractions is to have separate notebook just for them. When I am praying and focusing on God and a distraction comes up, I write it down in the journal on the left and get right back to prayer.

In my prayer time, God gives me information and marching orders for the day. Sometimes he gives me names and phone numbers of people I am supposed to call. Frequently it is just a name and instructions to pray for them. Other times I am just there, in his presence worshipping God. Sometimes he is giving me advice on an investment to make or a business to buy or sell. Sometimes he wants me to give a specific amount to a specific person at a specific time with a message for that person to remind them that God is real and cares about their lives.

When I am done with my prayer time, I have a list of things God wants me to do and a bunch of ideas that have made it into my journal. As I exit the prayer closet my assistants are standing by for a quick staff meeting on the deck. We have another round of coffee and light refreshments while I disseminate information and instructions to the different assistants. We have several business ventures and many clients in our consulting business and God is always giving us direction in our business and insight into the business of our clients.

I pray "God if this is your will for my life throw the doors open wide, if this is not your will God, please slam the door shut." As a human being this is a difficult thing to do. Sometimes the business profits look so good and easy it is really hard to shake a stick at it when God slams the doors shut. (I have had meetings with multi-millionaires that have been cancelled just after these prayers. I may never know the problems God had spared me from by slamming those doors shut.)

In my perfect day this continues with family time at the breakfast table. We are joined by out of town guests who are staying in our very large home. Some of these guests are dignitaries and others are friends we have met while travelling the world. There is sightseeing and fun activities through the day. I travel for speaking engagements and bring family and friends along for the experience. That is my "Perfect Day Exercise" and I have been doing it since the hospital. Many of those things have come true. You can write your own perfect day. Uplift and edify yourself with forward thinking and use your words to command your future.

Think about it…

Right now, take out a piece of paper or use this blank space to write down how your life would be different…

Do it now…

"if all things were possible how would your life be different?"

The future is bright, if you think you can you can, if you think you can't, you can't. Decide right now that you are going to…

Get STARTED and don't quit!

Describe your perfect day...

Get STARTED-don't quit!

Describe your perfect day…

179

www.GetSTARTED-dontquit.com

Get STARTED-don't quit!

Describe your perfect day…